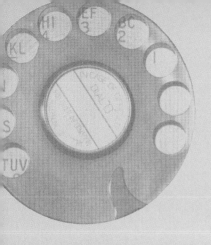

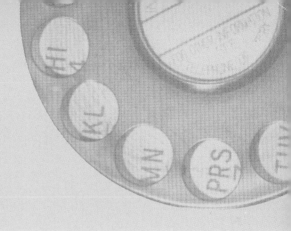

The Telephone

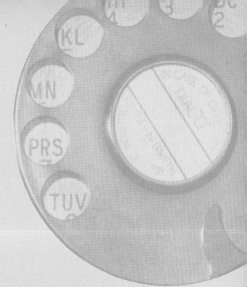

GREAT INVENTIONS

The Telephone

REBECCA STEFOFF

Marshall Cavendish
Benchmark
New York

Marshall Cavendish Benchmark
99 White Plains Road
Tarrytown, NY 10591-9001
www.marshallcavendish.us

Library of Congress Cataloging-in-Publication Data

Stefoff, Rebecca
The telephone / by Rebecca Stefoff.
p. cm. — (Great inventions)
Includes bibliographical references and index.
ISBN 0-7614-1879-2
1. Telephone—Juvenile literature. I. Title. II. Series: Great
inventions (Benchmark Books (Firm)).

TK6165.S74 2005
621.385—dc22
2004022108

Series design by Sonia Chaghatzbanian

Photo research by Candlepants Incorporated

Cover photo: Phil Leo/Photographer's Choice/Getty Images

The photographs in this book are used by permission and through the courtesy of:
Photo Researchers Inc.: Sheila Terry, 2, 42 (top and lower), 51; SPL, 36.
Will & Demi McIntyre, 89. *Corbis:* 17, 32, 39, 53; Bettmann, 12, 18, 23, 26, 30, 34, 41,
44, 48, 56, 64, 71, 77, 80, 82, 85; Leonardo de Selva, 14; Minnesota Historical
Society, 68; Strauss/Curtis, 102; Rolf Bruderer, 104. *Getty Images:* 20, 78;
Hulton-Archives, 63 (lower), 66, 86, 97; Time-Life Pictures, 63 (top), 74,
108-110; Andrew Olney, 91; Photodisc Red, 100.

Printed in China

1 3 5 6 4 2

C O N T E N T S

The Telephone

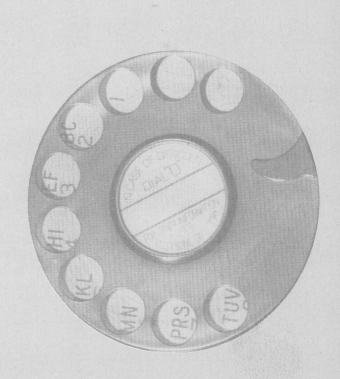

FOR MANY PEOPLE, THE CELLULAR TELEPHONE, OR CELL PHONE, HAS BECOME A VITAL COMMUNICATION TOOL. NOW PART OF EVERYDAY LIFE, TELEPHONES ALSO HELP SHAPE THE LARGER EVENTS OF HISTORY, AS IN THE CASE OF CALLS PLACED FROM A HIJACKED AIRLINER ON SEPTEMBER 11, 2001.

ONE

Breaking the Distance Barrier

More than two dozen telephone calls were made from an airplane as it flew over Ohio and western Pennsylvania on the morning of September 11, 2001. The plane was United Airlines Flight 93, a commercial airliner that had been hijacked by terrorists. The calls, made on cell phones, may have changed U.S. history.

Some of the thirty-seven passengers on the hijacked airplane had access to cellular telephones. Filled with confusion and fear, they used the phones to call loved ones and to seek help. The first call was from a passenger to his wife in California, telling her to alert the authorities. Another passenger, Todd Beamer of New Jersey, reached an emergency operator in Illinois. He reported that the hijackers had seized the cockpit and were flying the plane erratically. Other passengers also called family members, to reassure them or to bid them farewell. During these calls, the terrified passengers of Flight 93 learned what was happening elsewhere in the United States that morning. They were told that three other planes had also been hijacked, and that those planes had already been flown into buildings—two into the twin towers of New York City's World Trade Center and one into the Pentagon, the headquarters of the U.S. Defense Department in Washington, D.C.

Then the passengers and flight crew of Flight 93 knew that theirs was no ordinary hijacking, and that they had little or no chance of coming out of it alive. Their plane was headed southeast, toward Washington, D.C. Was its target the White House, home of the president, or the Capitol, the seat of Congress? No one knew.

Beamer told the emergency operator that he and several other men aboard the flight had decided to rush the hijacker who was guarding the passenger compartment—with a bomb strapped around his waist. The last words the operator heard from Beamer were, "Are you ready? Let's roll." A short time later, Flight 93 crashed into a field in western Pennsylvania. Did the passengers overwhelm their captors and cause the crash to avert a disaster in Washingon? No one knows for certain. All aboard Flight 93 were killed, but no one else was. The telephone had given the passengers vital information about their situation—and, thanks to the telephone, we know about the heroic action they took as a result.

The calls that connected Flight 93 during its last minutes to the rest of the country were part of a complex web of long-distance communications that encircles the Earth. Many elements are woven into the web—from splintered telephone poles lining country roads to high-tech telecommunications satellites gliding invisibly through space, from buried cables and looming relay towers to sleek pocket-sized devices that carry voices, images, or messages around the world in an instant. This long-distance communications web grew out of a world-changing invention: the telephone, created in 1876 by a restlessly inquisitive creative genius named Alexander Graham Bell. With the invention of the telephone, for the first time people separated by distance could hold a conversation.

The telephone revolutionized communication as much as the printing press had centuries earlier or the personal computer and the Internet a century later. It affected almost every aspect of life. People found new kinds of jobs as telephone operators, installers, and technicians. Manners, customs, business practices, even social relationships changed as the influence of the telephone became universal. That influence keeps evolving. Seventy years ago, people fretted about the proper etiquette for party lines, group telephone lines that were sometimes shared by as many as twenty households. Although the party line is now a thing of the past, today society grapples with new issues, such as rules and customs for using cell phones in public places, or laws that protect or invade the privacy of telephone conversations.

"Most extraordinary," said England's Queen Victoria in 1877, after Bell had demonstrated his invention to her. But the telephone was not really so extraordinary. It was a natural outgrowth of the scientific interests and advances of Bell's time, including discoveries about electricity and other inventions, such as the telegraph. Many people were trying to invent a telephone. More than one of them succeeded. A rival inventor almost beat Bell to the punch—or to the ring. All of these inventors were seeking a new solution to an age-old problem: how to communicate over distance.

People have used all sorts of methods for transmitting their words. The original method, of course, was simply talking—or shouting, if the listener was too far away for normal conversation. Over greater distances, messengers could carry news. Many societies developed postal services to deliver written messages. Some postal systems used fast runners or riders to carry mail or messages at high speeds. Under the right conditions, such systems could be remarkably efficient. For a short period in the early 1860s, for example, the Pony Express set overland speed records with the rapid relay of its riders on fast horses in the American West. Pony Express couriers could carry 20-pound (9.1-kilogram) mailbags over the 1,966 miles (3,164 kilometers) between Saint Joseph, Missouri, and Sacramento, California, in as little as eight days. The farthest-reaching, longest-lasting relay system was introduced in Asia in the thirteenth century, under the Mongol emperor Chingis, or Genghis, Khan. Horsemen carried his imperial messages to all corners of his realm, routinely covering distances of more than 250 miles (403 kilometers) a day. The Mongol "horse-post" system, as it was called, was so efficient that it remained in use in parts of the former empire until the middle of the twentieth century.

But what if you wanted or needed to send a message faster than even

PONY EXPRESS RIDERS, MANY OF THEM TEENAGERS, BECAME SYMBOLS OF THE DARING AND COURAGE OF THE AMERICAN WEST. YET THE OVERLAND-MAIL SERVICE EXISTED FOR LESS THAN TWO YEARS BEFORE THE TELEGRAPH—FORERUNNER OF THE TELEPHONE—PUT IT OUT OF BUSINESS.

the fastest runner or rider could carry it? Since ancient times, people have solved that problem in two basic ways: with sounds and with visual signals. Sound-based signaling systems have used drums, whistles, and fireworks. The earliest known visual signals were fires. Their smoke could be seen from far away by day, and the flames served as beacons or signals, especially at night, when they were more visible. As early as 430 B.C.E., the ancient Greeks had taken the concept of the beacon fire a step further. To send urgent military messages in a time of war, they stationed soldiers on hilltops and equipped them with torches. By waving combinations of torches in certain patterns, the soldiers could send coded messages. In later centuries, another communications technique appeared. Called heliography, from the Greek words for "sun" and "writing," it used glass or metal mirrors to reflect sunlight, flashing signals that could be seen from a distance if they were properly aimed.

In 1683 the city of Vienna almost fell to a besieging Turkish army. Europeans' anxiety about the event led an English physicist named Robert Hooke to consider ways in which urgent news could be communicated quickly to whole countries. By the next year, he had outlined a system involving large wooden frames placed on hilltops or other high points. Signalers could hang letters, symbols, or numbers on the frames to spell out a message; spotters at the next station would read the message through a telescope and pass it on. Hooke's system is called an optical telegraph, although Hooke never used the term. *Telegraph* comes from the Greek words for "far writing" or "writing at a distance."

Hooke's optical telegraph was never widely used, but in 1794 a French engineer named Claude Chappe devised a similar system that grew into a long-distance communications network. Once again, war and the urgent need for rapid military communication inspired the inventor: France was embroiled in the conflicts that followed the French Revolution of 1789. Chappe's system was based on semaphore signaling, long used for communication among ships at sea. By holding colored flags in a series of positions, a seaman on one ship could send a coded message to another vessel—if it was close enough to see the signals.

An early model of Claude Chappe's optical telegraph, which would soon send messages across France. When Napoléon Bonaparte seized control of the capital in 1799, he used Chappe's system to send these reassuring words to the rest of the country: "Paris is quiet and the good citizens are content."

Chappe adapted semaphoring to land use. Instead of using flags, he built a signal that consisted of three pieces of wood fastened together by movable joints. The operator pulled on a set of cords to arrange the three parts of the signal into a series of shapes. An alphabet was quickly created, with a distinctive shape for each letter and number. Once an operator had learned the code, he could send and receive messages almost as quickly as they could be written down. Lines of signaling stations, each relaying the message to the next, made the optical telegraph effective over great distances. The French adopted Chappe's system and quickly installed signaling stations in hundreds of high places with good visibility, including hills and mountains, the tops of existing buildings, and specially built towers. By the early 1840s, a network of more than five hundred signaling stations linked twenty-nine French cities. On a clear, sunny day, a message could travel from the capital city of Paris to the Mediterranean port of Toulon, 500 miles (805 kilometers) away, in about twenty minutes.

By that time, variations of Chappe's design had cropped up in a few places. In Great Britain, a line of signaling stations linked London with the coastal city of Dover. The system had been built to carry foreign news, brought to Dover on ships, swiftly to the capital. During the early years of the nineteenth century, important news was usually about military subjects—Britain and France were fighting one another on sea and land as part of the Napoleonic Wars. In 1815 the British and their allies, the Prussians, met the French army of Napoléon Bonaparte in a decisive battle at Waterloo in Belgium. When a ship reached Dover with word of a British victory, signalers immediately began relaying the glorious news to London. But a heavy fog formed, preventing Londoners from seeing the signals. They had to wait until a messenger arrived on horseback.

This inability to inform the worried Londoners is a perfect example of the shortcomings of the optical telegraph. The early systems of long-distance signaling were ingenious and useful, but all of them had drawbacks. Some could not be used at night or in bad weather. Because interpreters or signalers were needed to relay messages, human error caused many in-accuracies, especially over a large number of stages. And all of the early methods of long-distance communication were best suited to simple mes-sages. It is difficult and time consuming to send a complicated or lengthy message using drumbeats, flashes of sunlight, or coded signals. Some-thing better was needed—something that would let people communicate in detail and at length, quickly and in all conditions.

Two goals tantalized inventors. One goal was a rapid, reliable round-the-clock way to send written or coded messages across great dis-tances—perhaps even across an ocean. The other was the transmission of the human voice, so that people could speak directly to one another even when far apart. Although these two quests would one day merge into a unified program of long-distance communications, for a time they led researchers in different directions.

Perhaps Robert Hooke should be considered the founding father of telecommunications. In addition to inventing the first known optical telegraph, Hooke also launched a line of research into sending sounds over distances. Hooke was deeply interested in acoustics, or the physical properties of sound. He conducted many experiments to determine how sound travels through various materials, such as air, string, and wire. Among other things, he demonstrated that sound travels along strings and wires, even—Hooke reported with amazement—around corners.

Hooke was an inventor as well as an experimenter. One of Hooke's inventions was designed to help people who were hard of hearing—not the completely deaf, but those with minor or partial hearing loss. He demonstrated it to the Royal Society, England's leading association of learned and scientific minds. The society's archives record that on April 16, 1668, "Mr. Hooke produced again the large conical tin receiver for the magnifying of sounds; which being tried was found to make words softly uttered at a distance to be heard distinctly; whereas they could not be so heard without this instrument." Hooke's "tin receiver" was an early form of the device that came to be called an ear trumpet, which some people continued to use until the invention of the hearing aid in

Developed by Robert Hooke in the mid-seventeenth century, the ear trumpet was a form of hearing aid for the partially deaf that remained in use for several hundred years. People carried their ear trumpets around with them in leather or embroidered cases.

ALESSANDRO VOLTA RECEIVED MANY INTERNATIONAL SCIENTIFIC AWARDS FOR HIS INVENTION OF THE VOLTAIC PILE, THE FIRST ELECTRIC BATTERY. HIS DISCOVERY OF A RELIABLE POWER SOURCE TRANS-FORMED THE WORLD, MAKING POSSIBLE A HOST OF OTHER INVENTIONS, INCLUDING THE TELEPHONE.

the twentieth century. With the narrow end of the cone-shaped trumpet placed near the ear, the bell-shaped wide end gathered and amplified sounds and funneled them into the ear. As Hooke discovered, the ear trumpet works both ways. Just as listening through the narrow end made distant or faint sounds easier to hear, speaking or shouting into the narrow end amplified the sounds that came out of the wide end. Used this way, the device becomes a megaphone for projecting the voice.

A few years after his demonstration to the Royal Society, Hooke created an instrument that combined the ear trumpet with his findings about the sound-carrying properties of strings. He connected two cylinders with a line. As anyone who has ever played with two empty soup cans and a taut string can confirm, sounds made into one end of the instrument can be heard through the other end. Hooke developed the string telephone as part of his research into making and transmitting music. We cannot tell from his notes whether he viewed it as a tool for spoken communication. Still, it is clearly an ancestor of the telephone. But the true telephone would not appear for many years, and it would not be the first form of high-speed long-distance communication. Written words, not spoken ones, would be the first to flash across the miles.

From time to time during the early nineteenth century, the U.S. Congress debated whether or not it should build an optical telegraph system like the one that was spreading across France. Americans who visited France came home with tales of the marvelous speed with which signalers could send important news over great distances. By the 1830s many government and business leaders in the United States were clamoring for such a network. According to some historians, Congress might very well have authorized and paid for one, except for one thing—a different, better kind of telegraph soon became available. This new telegraph did not depend on fickle daylight. It was driven by a newly understood force that was gaining importance not just in scientific circles but in other areas of life as well: electricity.

As early as 1753, in the journal *Scots Magazine,* an anonymous writer had outlined an idea for an electrical telegraph, one that would

ALTHOUGH SAMUEL F. B. MORSE STARTED OUT AS A PAINTER, HIS PLACE IN HISTORY RESTS ON HIS INVENTION OF THE DEVICE HE HOLDS HERE: THE TELEGRAPH. HE ALSO CREATED THE MORSE CODE, A NEW ALPHABET FOR USE IN TELEGRAPHING.

have a separate wire for each letter of the alphabet. Electrical current could be sent along various wires in sequence, spelling out a message. The idea soon became reality. Between 1774 and 1830, inventors in Switzerland, France, Germany, Spain, England, and the United States developed many versions of the multi-wire telegraph. These early telegraph systems were not large-scale communications systems. They were more like experiments-in-progress or demonstrations. Their power sources were erratic and unreliable—scientists, after all, were still working out the basic principles of electricity and how to harness it. And the distances covered by the early telegraphs were small. One of the longer lines ran for 8 miles (almost 13 kilometers), but most just went from one building or room to the next. Still, they showed clearly that the electrical telegraph had great potential for fast communication.

Power ceased to be a real problem after 1800. That year an Italian scientist named Alessandro Volta introduced the voltaic pile, the first electric battery. Made of alternating disks of silver and zinc, with brine-soaked felt pads between them, the battery was a compact, reliable source of steady electrical current. Telegraphers then had to find a convenient way to use that current to communicate. How could they turn words into electrically powered signals at one end of the line—and then back into words again at the other?

Telegraphers answered that question in an impressive variety of ways. In the so-called bubble telegraph, the current activated a chemical solution at the receiving end, releasing bubbles of hydrogen, one for each letter of a message. In other systems, sparks flashed or bells rang at the receiving ends of the alphabet wires. But soon another important discovery in electrical science led to innovations in signaling. In 1819 a Danish physicist named Hans Christian Oersted discovered that an electrical current passing through a wire would cause a nearby magnetic needle to move. At once a number of scientists and engineers, including André-Marie Ampère in France and Michael Faraday in England, began studying the properties of electromagnetism. Inventors quickly adapted the newly discovered electromagnet to telegraphy. In England, William Cooke and Charles Wheatstone developed an instrument that laid the foundations of the British commercial telegraph industry. The sending operator opened and closed the electrical current, causing a magnetized needle to move at the other end of the line. These movements could convey messages in a code that Cooke and Wheatstone created.

On the other side of the Atlantic Ocean, an American scientist and teacher named Joseph Henry also developed an electromagnetic signaling instrument. In 1831 he demonstrated it in a classroom. He wrapped a wire repeatedly around a magnet. Near the magnet, he positioned a movable steel bar on a small pivot. Next to the bar stood a bell. Henry then touched both ends of the wire to a battery, closing the electrical circuit. As soon as he did so, electromagnetism pulled the steel bar, which moved and struck the bell, causing it to ring. When Henry took the wires away from the battery, breaking the circuit, the bar returned to its original position. He could make it ring as many times as he wanted by closing and breaking the circuit repeatedly.

But although Henry had invented a simple, practical telegraph based on an electrical signal, he did not register it with the U.S. Patent Office in order to prevent others from duplicating and profiting from his invention. Henry not only did not bother to patent his invention, he did not attempt to develop it into a business. Those achievements belong to an artist named Samuel Finley Breese Morse.

Born in Massachusetts in 1791, Morse trained as a painter. Later he became moderately well known for his portraits. He settled in New York City, where he became friendly with the city's elite and was the founder and first president of the National Academy of Design. In the early 1830s Morse heard about electromagnetism and came up with the idea of an electromagnetic telegraph. Although he had no scientific training and had showed no previous interest in engineering or experimentation, he began working to turn his idea into reality. The telegraph was not a single-minded obsession for Morse, who was also busy painting, teaching art, and dabbling in local politics. But by 1836, he had made a working model of his telegraph. Instead of ringing a bell like Henry's device, Morse's telegraph used electromagnetism to move a

A WESTERN UNION OPERATING ROOM IN 1881. TELEGRAPHY, THE FIRST FORM OF RAPID LONG-DISTANCE COMMUNICATION, WAS BIG BUSINESS, BUT THE NEWLY INVENTED TELEPHONE WAS ABOUT TO CHANGE THAT.

marker that made short marks (dots) and longer ones (dashes) on a moving strip of paper. Morse created a code that used a unique combination of dots and dashes for each letter and number; the Morse code is still used today. The artist-turned-inventor soon became an entrepreneur. He acquired business partners and tried to convince Congress to pay him to build a telegraph line.

Morse tried to get his business off the ground in Europe as well as in the United States. He had no luck abroad, where other inventors had patented similar devices and were lobbying for their own systems. But in the United States he found a new partner in a congressman from Maine. With that official's help, he finally persuaded the U.S. Congress to build the first American telegraph line—linking Baltimore, Maryland, and Washington, D.C.—in 1844. The first message sent across it was solemn and ceremonial: "What hath God wrought?"

What Morse had wrought was a revolution in communication. Soon Morse was licensing his invention to telegraph companies all over the country. One of the largest of these companies was Western Union. By 1851 it was swallowing up other smaller companies, on the way to building a national communications network owned by one company. Western Union offices sprang up everywhere, offering quick communication both between cities and within them. Employees encoded customers' messages into dots and dashes and sent them over the lines in the form of telegrams. Workers at the receiving end decoded the telegrams, which were then either delivered to or picked up by the recipients. When Western Union found that workers could decode sounds more quickly than printed dots and dashes, telegraph equipment was modified to use sounders, devices that made short and long buzzing or clicking noises. Later, automatic decoders speeded up the process even more.

In 1861 Western Union completed the first transcontinental telegraph line, linking the nation's two coasts—and putting the short-lived Pony Express out of business. Five years later, after several failed attempts, a telegraph line was laid on the floor of the Atlantic Ocean between Canada and England, allowing rapid communication between continents. On land, the poles that carried telegraph wires were becoming a common sight in urban and rural landscapes. Telegraphy was a big, booming business. It was also an increasingly familiar part of every-day life, as people grew used to communicating with business associates and family members faster than ever before.

The telegraph paved the way for the telephone in two ways. First, it showed that long-distance, electrically based communication over connecting wires was possible, practical, and popular. Second, it inspired the leading inventors of the time to search for ways to improve the telegraph. That search led one man to an entirely different instrument: the telephone. Instead of perfecting a better way to send written messages across the miles, Alexander Graham Bell would realize a different goal. He would send the human voice.

Sir Charles Wheatstone, a respected scientist and inventor, made a fortune in the British telegraph industry. When he demonstrated his "talking machine" to the teenaged Alexander Graham Bell, though, he planted a seed that would eventually produce a rival industry: the Bell Telephone Company.

Bell's Quest

In the mid-nineteenth century, Sir Charles Wheatstone was one of the most famous scientists in Great Britain. He was a partner in the most successful telegraph company in the United Kingdom and an inventor of musical instruments and other devices. One day in 1861, two men visited Wheatstone at his London home. They were Alexander Melville Bell and his son, a mature and thoughtful young man of fourteen who was named Alexander Bell but was always called Aleck. They had come to see one of Wheatstone's creations: a machine that could speak words.

Many people were building such machines at the time—or claiming to. These machines often appeared as entertainments at fairs. Most were tricks, operated by ventriloquism or fraud. But Wheatstone's construction was a set of chambers, tubes, and movable parts that imitated the structure of the human throat and mouth. With the pieces that duplicated the tongue and lips set into position, Wheatstone used a bellows to force air through the machine. To young Aleck's astonishment, the device seemed to speak. Years later he recalled the importance of that moment: "I saw Sir Charles manipulate the machine and heard it speak, and although the articulation was disappointingly crude, it made a great impression on my mind."

When the Bells returned to their home in Edinburgh, Scotland,

Aleck and his older brother, Melville, decided to make a speaking machine of their own. "[Melville] undertook to make the lungs and throat of the apparatus," Bell wrote, "while I made the tongue and mouth." The boys' creation, crafted of rubber, cotton, wood, wire, and a bellows, was hardly attractive, but it was effective. Aleck and Melville tested it in a stairway shared by the Bells and their neighbors. Long afterward, Alexander Graham Bell recalled that the device "really sounded like a baby in great distress. 'Mamma, Mamma' came forth with heart-rending effect. We heard someone above say, 'Good gracious, what can be the matter with that baby,' and then footsteps were heard. This, of course, was just what we wanted. We quietly slipped into our house, and closed the door, leaving our neighbours to pursue their fruitless quest for the baby." More than forty years later, Bell wrote, "The making of this talking-machine certainly marked an important point in my career. It made me familiar with the functions of the vocal cords, and started me along the path that led to the telephone."

One of the best biographies of Bell is Robert V. Bruce's *Bell: Alexander Graham Bell and the Conquest of Solitude.* At first glance, it might seem that the phrase *conquest of solitude* refers to Bell's most famous achievement, the telephone, which put an end to isolation and made it easier than ever for people to communicate. Yet for years Bell fought solitude on a more basic level—he worked to help end the solitude of the deaf. He was an expert in human speech, a subject in which his family had specialized for two generations before him.

Aleck's grandfather Alexander Bell was an actor. Later in his career he taught elocution, the art of correct and effective speaking, in London. In addition to giving public lectures, he gave private lessons to people who stammered, lisped, or were troubled with other speech defects. Aleck's father, Alexander Melville Bell, also became an elocution teacher. Known as Melville Bell, he wrote a number of highly influential textbooks and other works on pronunciation and the mechanics of human speech. His best-known book, *The Standard Elocutionist,* became something of a best seller. A quarter of a million copies were sold in the

United States and even more in England. The well-known playwright George Bernard Shaw mentioned "the illustrious Alexander Melville Bell" in the preface to his play *Pygmalion,* the story of a London professor who takes on the challenge of "correcting" the Cockney dialect of a street girl. Some scholars have suggested that Shaw's Professor Henry Higgins was inspired in part by Bell.

Aleck Bell, the second of Melville Bell's three sons, was born in Edinburgh in 1847. At the age of eleven, Aleck chose the middle name Graham for himself as a way of setting his name apart from his father's and grandfather's, and afterward he often signed his name "A Graham Bell." But if Aleck's choice of name was a sign of an independent spirit, he remained closely linked to the family in his choice of occupation. Although as a child he enjoyed an excellent education in music and dreamed of becoming a professional musician, Aleck grew deeply interested in his father's work.

While Aleck was growing up, Melville Bell was engaged in a fifteen-year research project. He wanted to identify and describe every sound that the human organs of speech could possibly make. Like other elocutionists and speech scholars of his day, Bell hoped to develop a universal alphabet, a set of symbols that would represent every sound in any of the world's many languages. If all sounds could be clearly written down so that anyone could pronounce them, not only would people find it much easier to speak foreign languages properly, but scholars and explorers would be able to make accurate records of rare and exotic languages. In time, Melville Bell created just such a universal alphabet—a set of symbols to describe the position and movements of the tongue and lips while the speaker was uttering any of the possible sounds. Bell called his system Visible Speech.

Aleck and his brother Melville helped their father demonstrate Visible Speech at lectures. The elder Bell would send the boys out of the room and then invite the audience to come up with difficult sounds or obscure foreign words. Bell would then write the sound or word on a blackboard, using the symbols of Visible Speech. Upon returning to the

MELVILLE BELL'S VISIBLE SPEECH SYSTEM EVOLVED INTO NEW FORMS OVER THE YEARS. BY 1945 IT HAD BECOME A DEVICE THAT TRANSLATED SOUNDS INTO PATTERNS OF LIGHT THAT APPEARED ON SCREENS, DEMONSTRATED HERE AT THE BELL LABORATORIES.

room, the boys—well schooled in the alphabet their father had invented—reproduced the sounds and words perfectly.

Melville Bell realized that Visible Speech had possibilities beyond language scholarship and elocution training. It might help the deaf learn to speak. Deafness had touched the Bell family—Aleck's mother, Eliza Bell, had gradually lost much of her ability to hear. She was not completely deaf. She used a hearing tube, a descendant of Hooke's ear trumpet, to amplify sounds and voices, even pressing it to the piano so that she could hear the music when she or Aleck played.

Eliza Bell spoke perfectly well. But people who had been deaf since birth found it extremely difficult to learn how to speak clearly and understandably. Unable to hear others or themselves, they could only imitate the visible facial movements of other people. As a result, the sounds they made could be impossible for others to understand. But Visible Speech, with its sound symbols, presented words in terms of mouth positions and movements. A deaf person could learn to pronounce words by "reading" them in Visible Speech. As Melville Bell worked to complete and fine-tune his system, he also began trying to interest schools and the British government in it as an educational tool for the deaf. During a trip to the United States to drum up support for Visible Speech, Bell met Gardiner Greene Hubbard, a Boston attorney who had a deaf daughter. Hubbard was helping to support a school for the deaf. His meeting with Melville Bell would play a crucial role in Aleck Bell's future.

Well before Melville Bell's book on Visible Speech was published in 1867, young Aleck had begun his own professional career as a teacher. At the age of sixteen, he taught music and elocution to students, some of them older than himself, at a school called Elgin's Weston House Academy, not far from Edinburgh. He then took some courses at the University of Edinburgh before becoming a full-time teacher. One of his father's former pupils now operated a school for the deaf in London, and at her request Aleck Bell began teaching children there, using the Visible

GERMAN PHILOSOPHER AND SCIENTIST HERMANN VON HELMHOLTZ RESEARCHED BOTH SIGHT AND SOUND AS WELL AS MANY OTHER FIELDS, FROM WEATHER TO ELECTRICITY. HIS STUDIES OF THE MECHANISM OF THE EAR AND THE PRINCIPLES OF ACOUSTICS INSPIRED BELL, EVEN THOUGH BELL MISUNDERSTOOD A KEY DETAIL OF HELMHOLTZ'S WORK.

Speech method. He was a great success as a teacher. Later he said that the experience launched him on what he called his "life-work—the teaching of speech to the deaf."

Bell also pursued his own research into the phenomena of sound and speech. Like his father, he conducted experiments and recorded the results. Using thin stretched membranes, he studied the vibrations in the air made by different sounds. Around this time, Bell read the work of Hermann von Helmholtz, a German scientist who had published a book on sound in 1863. Helmholtz had studied the musical properties of vowel sounds by using tuning forks—tools often used by piano tuners to adjust the sounds of the instruments. To make his investigations easier, Helmholtz had kept the forks vibrating by attaching them to battery-powered electromagnets. Bell read Helmholtz's work but misinterpreted it—he thought that the German was actually transmitting vowel sounds through the air with the use of electricity. Although that was not the case, the concepts of sound transmission and electricity became linked in Bell's mind. He began thinking about the possibility of "talking by telegraph," as he put it, and he started studying electricity, batteries, and telegraph equipment.

Tragedy struck the Bell family in 1867, when Aleck's younger brother died of tuberculosis. Three years later his older brother died of the same disease. Melville and Eliza Bell decided to emigrate with their remaining son to Canada, where they hoped that Melville's Visible

Speech program would prosper and the climate would keep Aleck healthy. By late 1870 the family had settled in Brantford, Ontario. Aleck Bell did not stay there for long, however. His father arranged a series of two- and three-month teaching positions for him at schools for the deaf across New England. In 1872 the younger Bell settled in Boston, which he called "the intellectual centre of the States," and began teaching deaf pupils, both privately and at Boston University. One of his pupils was the son of a wealthy leather merchant named Thomas Sanders, in whose house Bell lived for several years. Later Bell also tutored Mabel Hubbard, the daughter of the lawyer Gardiner Greene Hubbard, president of a school for the deaf. The teenaged Mabel was not impressed with the earnest young Scotsman. "I did not like him," she said. "He was tall and dark, with jet black hair and eyes, but dressed badly and carelessly in an old-fashioned suit. . . ."

Busy as he was teaching the deaf and promoting Visible Speech, Bell continued his investigations into sound and electricity, attending scientific lectures and reading books on the subjects. By this time his interest was no longer purely scholarly. Bell was itching to invent something.

The inventive spirit had gripped the era. The previous few decades had produced a spate of new processes and products, including dynamite, refrigeration, machine guns, new forms of steel and concrete, and the first electric lightbulbs and internal-combustion engines. "The greatest invention of the nineteenth century," wrote English philosopher Alfred North Whitehead, "was the invention of the method of invention." People in Europe and North America felt that they were living in an age of progress and scientific wonders.

Telegraphy was one of those wonders. But many felt that telegraphy could be improved. With the growing volume of telegraphic communication, people were looking for a way to send multiple messages across the same telegraph wire at the same time. Several people—including a young American named Thomas Alva Edison, born in the same year as Bell—were working on the problem. Edison succeeded in inventing a duplex telegraph, one that could transmit two messages at once. So did

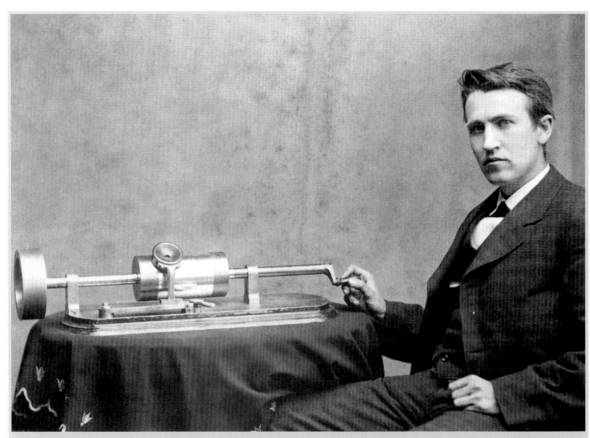

One of Bell's leading rivals in the race to develop a telegraph that could send multiple messages at the same time was Thomas A. Edison, shown here with one of his many inventions, the phonograph or record player. Later, when the telephone business was forming, Edison established a partnership with Bell's chief competitor.

another inventor named Joseph Stearns, who beat Edison to the market. In October 1872 Alexander Graham Bell read in the newspaper that Western Union had paid a large sum for Stearns's invention. The next month, convinced that an even greater reward awaited the inventor who found a way to send still more messages simultaneously, Bell began a program of research and experimentation in his rooms in the Sanders house. He wanted to produce something called a "harmonic telegraph"—a machine that would use different musical notes to send multiple messages simultaneously along a telegraph wire. Bell devoted tremendous energy and thought to this quest, which would soon lead him in a new and unexpected direction.

ALEXANDER GRAHAM BELL IS BEST KNOWN TODAY AS THE INVENTOR OF THE TELEPHONE, BUT HE THOUGHT THE MOST IMPORTANT WORK OF HIS LIFE WAS IMPROVING COMMUNICATION FOR THE DEAF.

THREE

Bell's Triumph

More than scientific curiosity and a desire to benefit humanity drove Alexander Graham Bell's urge to create. Bell was also eager to improve his financial standing. He knew that some inventors had made great fortunes. Recognizing the potential profits to be gained by the first person to develop a harmonic telegraph, he guarded his work carefully, locking away his notes and equipment when he was not working on them. His focus was on a telegraph-like device using thin, flexible steel reeds that would vibrate at the frequencies of different musical notes.

While Bell worked on his harmonic telegraph, he was teaching and lecturing about sound, speech, and hearing. He was also experimenting with devices to transmit sounds. A colleague at Boston University gave him a human ear, taken from a dead man, for his experiments. Bell attached the membrane of the ear to a pencil-like marker that moved across a paper when the vibrations of spoken words struck the membrane. This device showed Bell that a membrane could respond to very small and subtle differences in the pitch and frequency of sounds. He began thinking about a machine that would use a single membrane, rather than an array of reeds, to reproduce the effects of sound.

By the spring of 1874, when Bell left to spend the summer with his parents in Canada, he knew that an inventor named Elisha Gray, who was sponsored by Western Union, was also striving to create a harmonic telegraph. Gray had already succeeded in transmitting eight musical tones through a wire—but not simultaneously. To protect his interests, Bell tried to file a patent caveat for the harmonic telegraph. A caveat is not a final patent, simply a formal notice that an invention is under way. The U.S. Patent Office, however, notified Bell that because he was not an American citizen, he could not file a caveat. All he could do was complete his harmonic telegraph and patent the final invention.

This setback discouraged Bell. Yet the harmonic telegraph was not his only project. He had grown increasingly interested in a different, though related, line of research concerning sound transmission. His studies of the ear membrane had shown the power of sound vibrations to move physical objects. He concluded that if an electrical current linked two membranes, words spoken into one of them would cause that membrane to vibrate. This in turn would modulate, or change, the electrical current. As the changing current passed through the second membrane, it would set that membrane vibrating, echoing the sounds that had been spoken into the first one. Bell's growing knowledge of electricity, vibrating membranes, and the physical properties of sound had come together—a marriage of concepts that would eventually lead to the telephone.

Back in Boston in the fall, Bell was eager to pursue his idea of a speaking machine. But experimentation was costly. Bell needed electrical equipment, other supplies, and an assistant to help with the technical work. He found two financial backers in Thomas Sanders and Gardiner Greene Hubbard, whose deaf children had benefited from Bell's teaching. They formed a partnership that historians have named the Bell Patent Association, in which Bell did the work and Sanders and Hubbard provided the money. Bell's new partners were specifically interested in his harmonic telegraph, an invention that was familiar to them, and one that offered immediate practical and commercial benefits. They urged Bell to hurry up and perfect the harmonic telegraph so that he could patent it, warning him frequently of the danger that Elisha Gray or some other unknown inventor would reach the prize first.

On November 23, 1874, Bell wrote to his parents, "It is a neck and neck race between Mr. Gray and myself who shall complete our apparatus first." By "apparatus," he meant the harmonic or multiple telegraph. But in that same letter, Bell shared his excitement about his other idea, which he had not yet given a name. He called it "an instrument by which the human voice might be telegraphed."

Soon Bell found someone to share his excitement about this new idea. In early 1875 a young man named Thomas Watson, an employee at a local firm that made and sold electrical equipment and supplies, began helping Bell with his experiments. Watson, a skilled electrician and machinist, proved a most valuable assistant.

IN 1931 THOMAS WATSON HOLDS A MODEL OF BELL'S TELEPHONE. MANY YEARS EARLIER, AS AN EAGER YOUNG ELECTRICIAN, WATSON HAD HELPED CREATE THAT INSTRUMENT. IN THE PROCESS, HE AND BELL HAD BECOME FRIENDS—A RELATIONSHIP THAT WOULD OUTLAST THEIR BUSINESS ASSOCIATION.

Within a year and a half, Watson had become a partner in the Bell Patent Association. He also became Bell's friend and trusted confidant. One day, as they worked together on Bell's harmonic telegraph—which still did not operate consistently in practical tests—Bell said, "Watson, if

I can get a mechanism which will make a current of electricity vary in its intensity, as the air varies in density when a sound is passing through it, I can telegraph any sound, even the sound of speech."

In March 1875, Hubbard and Sanders sent Bell to Washington, D.C., to apply for a patent for the harmonic telegraph. While in Washington, Bell visited the Smithsonian Institution and met its secretary, Joseph Henry—the same physicist who had demonstrated the first working model of an electrical telegraph more than forty years earlier. Bell told Henry about his ideas for sending the human voice across a wire. The older scientist called Bell's idea "the germ of a great invention" and urged the younger man to "work at it." Bell left the meeting filled with elation about his pet idea.

Sanders and Hubbard, however, impatiently brushed aside Bell's desire to pursue the "talking telegraph" idea. They pressed him to keep working to improve his harmonic or multiple telegraph, and he dutifully did so. He even demonstrated his multiple telegraph model to the heads of Western Union, although at the time it was effective for only two channels, like Stearns's machine. But Bell kept working, with Watson's help, to add more channels. That diligence led to an accidental breakthrough.

On June 2, the pair were in adjoining rooms, adjusting and tuning the steel reeds in two connected machines. Watson found that one of the reeds was screwed too tightly into place, and he started to loosen it. In doing so, he plucked at the reed, which gave off a faint, barely audible twang. From the next room, Bell shouted in surprise. The small noise had traveled along the wire to the receiver there—something that neither man had expected, because there was no current running through the wire from the battery. They realized at once that the energy of the sound itself had induced or created enough current, as it passed across the transmitter's electromagnet, to carry its signal to the next room. Watson later wrote, "[Bell] knew he was hearing, for the first

PHILIPP REIS IS SHOWN EXPERIMENTING WITH THE MACHINE THAT HE DUBBED A TELEPHON. THE DRAWING IS MISLEADING, HOWEVER. ALTHOUGH REIS APPEARS TO BE SPEAKING INTO HIS DEVICE, HE NEVER USED IT TO TRANSMIT SPEECH.

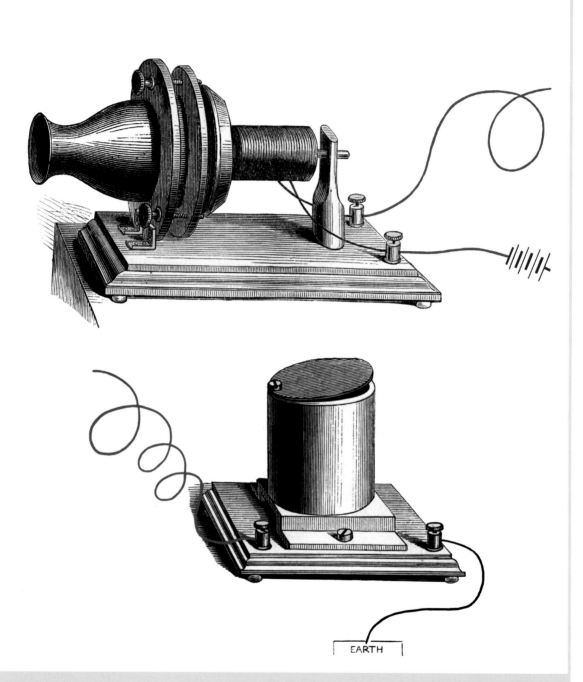

EARTH

BELL'S EARLY TELEPHONES WENT THROUGH A NUMBER OF DESIGN CHANGES. THE FIRST COMMERCIAL TELEPHONE WAS A SINGLE UNIT (TOP) THAT WAS BOTH A MOUTHPIECE FOR SPEAKING AND AN EARPIECE FOR LISTENING. BELL DEVELOPED SEVERAL VERSIONS OF THIS COMBINED TRANSMITTER/RECEIVER BEFORE SEPARATING THE FUNCTIONS INTO TWO UNITS, SO THAT CALLERS COULD SPEAK AND LISTEN AT THE SAME TIME. LATER, THE TRANSMITTER AND RECEIVER WOULD AGAIN BE COMBINED IN A SINGLE UNIT, WITH THE EARPIECE AT ONE END AND THE MOUTHPIECE AT THE OTHER. BUT WHEN DEMONSTRATING HIS INVENTION TO LARGE GROUPS OF PEOPLE, BELL USED A SPECIAL RECEIVER (BOTTOM) THAT PROJECTED THE MESSAGE INTO THE ROOM.

time in human history, the tones and overtones of a sound transmitted by electricity."

Watson was wrong. Bell was not the first to hear, or to send, a sound using an electromagnet. In 1861 a German educator named Philipp Reis had publicized his own invention—a machine that transmitted tones over a wire. Wrote Reis, "I named the instrument 'Telephon.'" Reis's machine did not transmit human speech, although with a few changes it could have been made to do so. But Reis never made those changes. He did not even claim that his machine could be used to send speech over wires. Reis's machine used an on-and-off electrical current, activated by closing and opening a circuit as in the telegraph—not the continuous current, shaped by the subtle tonal changes of the human voice, that Bell envisioned for his invention. Most important, Reis never tried to turn his instrument into a commercially useful product. For all of these reasons, most modern historians of technology view Reis's *Telephon*, along with similar devices created by other nineteenth-century inventors, as falling outside the direct chain of developments that led to true telephony.

The telephone as we know it was born when Bell heard that faint sound transmitted from the next room. He realized at once that he was on the verge of mastering "the transmission of the human voice." He quickly sketched a device built around the reeds used in the multiple telegraph and a membrane made of stretched parchment. Watson built it, and the two men tested it. It transmitted sound, but not clear spoken words. Although this first attempt had failed, Bell knew that he was close. He wrote to his parents, "I am like a man in a fog who is sure of his latitude and longitude. I know that I am close to the land for which I am bound and when the fog lifts I shall see it right before me."

Bell's backer Hubbard did nothing to help lift the fog. Still uninterested in the telephone, he urged Bell to keep working on the harmonic telegraph. Relations between the two men grew more complicated

BELL SPEAKS INTO THE EARLY TELEPHONE. RECEPTION ON THESE EARLY MACHINES WAS NOT ALWAYS GOOD—
MANY OF THE FIRST TELEPHONE MESSAGES CONSISTED OF PHRASES SUCH AS "SLOW DOWN, PLEASE," OR
"CAN YOU SPEAK MORE LOUDLY?"

when Bell fell suddenly and deeply in love with Mabel Hubbard, his deaf pupil, who was now seventeen. At first Mabel did not return his affection, but gradually her feelings for him warmed; in November, when she turned eighteen, the two became engaged. Their courtship caused a great strain between Bell and Gardiner Greene Hubbard, who insisted that Bell had to give up all other pursuits to work full-time on telegraphy if he wished to marry Mabel. But when Bell and Mabel defied Hubbard's heavy-handed interference, he reluctantly agreed to let both invention and romance take their own course.

Meanwhile, Bell had already prepared a design and description of the telephone suitable for a patent application. In early 1876 Hubbard and Sanders decided that they should protect Bell's new invention by patenting it—just in case it turned out to be worth something. They were dismayed to learn that Bell had already sold to a pair of Canadian businessmen the rights to patent and sell the invention in Great Britain. Bell had also agreed to delay applying for a telephone patent in the United States until the British patent had been secured. What he did not know was that the Canadians had lost interest in the machine and had not even tried to obtain the British patent. Hubbard grew frantic, fearing that Elisha Gray or another inventor would patent a telephone-like invention before Bell did. Finally, without telling Bell, Hubbard ordered his lawyers in Washington, D.C., to apply for a patent in Bell's name. They did so on the morning of February 14, 1876.

Hubbard's sneaky actions ultimately saved Bell's claim to the invention of the telephone. A few hours later on the same day, Elisha Gray showed up at the Patent Office to file a caveat on a very similar invention. After reviewing the two applications, the Patent Office decided that Bell's patent application had more merit than Gray's caveat application, as Bell's had been filed earlier and was for a completed invention. It issued the patent to Bell on March 7, 1876.

The word *telephone* does not even appear in Bell's patent application, which was titled "Improvement in Telegraphy." Nor did the application claim that the instrument transmitted human speech. Instead, it declared only that the apparatus transmitted "vocal or other sounds." But in it, Bell outlined several different methods of sound transmission in detail. One of them, involving a membrane and a modulated or variable current, became the basis for all later developments in telephony. Then all Bell had to do was protect his patent, make it profitable, and get his machine to work.

At the time of the patent application, Bell had not yet succeeded in sending understandable words over a wire. That milestone was reached three days after the patent was granted, on March 10. Bell and Watson were working in separate rooms, just as they had been when they had accidentally transmitted the sound of the vibrating reed. This time they were experimenting with a liquid transmitter, one in which the diaphragm or membrane was stretched on a frame over a cup of water with just enough acid in it to make it a good conductor of electrical current. An electrical line ran from the diaphragm into the liquid. Another line ran from the liquid through an electromagnet and on to the receiver in the other room. Bell theorized that speaking into the diaphragm would induce a current in the line, thus opening the electrical circuit. It would also create vibrations in the diaphragm that would move the transmitting wire up and down in the conducting liquid. Those movements would cause variations, or modulations, in the amount of current running through the circuit. At the receiving end, the variations in current would vibrate the other diaphragm in the receiver, duplicating the sounds that had been spoken into the transmitter.

Bell bent over his transmitter and spoke into it, speaking words that he and Watson later recalled, with slight differences, as, "Mr. Watson— come here—I want to see you." In the room separated from Bell by two closed doors, Watson clearly heard those words through the receiver.

Bell's telephone worked. He was exhilarated. That night he wrote to his parents that he foresaw a day when wires would run into each house, just like water pipes and gas lines, and "friends [could] converse with each other without leaving home."

PHILADELPHIA'S CENTENNIAL EXPOSITION OF 1876 DREW CROWDS OF PEOPLE WHO MARVELED AT THE MACHINERY AND OTHER SYMBOLS OF PROGRESS AND INVENTION. WITH A LITTLE HELP FROM THE EMPEROR OF BRAZIL, ALEXANDER GRAHAM BELL TURNED THE OCCASION INTO A TRIUMPH FOR HIS TELEPHONE.

FOUR

The Business of Communication

"I must confess . . . I don't see what good I can accomplish there," Bell wrote to Mabel in June 1876. He was on a train, bound for Philadelphia, where the Centennial Exhibition was under way. The exhibition was many things: a one-hundredth birthday party for the United States, a world's fair with pavilions from dozens of nations, and a celebration of technology and progress. Bell's new invention, the telephone, was included in a display of scientific and electrical gadgets.

Bell had not wanted to display the telephone—he felt it did not yet perform consistently and impressively enough to be unveiled to the public. Mabel and her father, however, had persuaded him. Bell had even agreed to go to Philadelphia to demonstrate his apparatus on June 25, when a panel of international scientists and dignitaries would judge the electrical exhibits. The occasion did not start off well for Bell and the telephone. The journey had damaged the telephone equipment, which had to be hastily repaired. The actual day of the judging was stiflingly hot; the judges, dressed in formal suits, visibly drooped as they paraded through the huge building from one exhibit to the next. But Elisha Gray's demonstration of his harmonic telegraph, which transmitted the musical notes of "Home, Sweet Home," filled them with excitement and awe. In the center of the main exhibition hall, Gray's invention was surrounded by an admiring crowd. Bell looked on. How could his telephone, tucked away in a bare room on another floor, possibly compete?

Unexpectedly, Bell received imperial aid. Dom Pedro II, the emperor of Brazil, was visiting the United States and had been in Boston two weeks earlier. There he had seen Bell demonstrate Visible Speech at Gardiner's school for the deaf. Now the emperor was attending the exhibition. He noticed Bell in the crowd and went to speak to him. Because Dom Pedro was one of the highest-ranking dignitaries present, the rest of the officials had no choice but to follow him, all the way upstairs, so that the emperor could examine Bell's invention. To Bell's great relief, the machine worked. From a separate room, the inventor spoke, sang, and recited speeches from Shakespeare's plays into the telephone transmitter, while the emperor and other witnesses, including the famous English scientist Sir William Thomson and rival inventor Elisha Gray, stood marveling around the receiver. Thomson called Bell's invention "the most wonderful thing" he had seen during his trip to the United States.

According to Thomson, the telephone was of "transcendent scientific interest." However, scientific interest did not pay the bills. It was time for Bell and his partners to turn the new invention into a money-making venture. But how could they do so?

Hubbard had already thought of one way. The Bell Patent Association could sell the invention to Western Union, which already had an extensive network of telegraph wires across the country. Just a few months after Bell's triumphant demonstration at the Centennial Exhibition, Hubbard offered to sell the telephone to Western Union for $100,000. William Orton, the company's president, turned down the offer—and earned the dubious honor of being remembered as "the man who refused to buy the most profitable invention in recorded history," as Edwin S. Grosvenor and Morgan Wesson wrote in *Alexander Graham Bell: The Life and Times of the Man Who Invented the Telephone*.

But profit seemed a long way off in late 1876 and early 1877. Bell was so broke that he had to borrow money from Watson to pay for some of his meals. Still, he was desperately eager to start making money so that he could get married. He and Watson began giving lectures about telephony. Although these events were educational, they were also a form of entertainment. People paid the admission fee chiefly to see the amazing new machine demonstrated. "My singing was always a hit," the unmelodious Watson wrote years later, tongue in cheek. "The telephone obscured its defects and gave it a mystic touch."

Problems were plentiful in early telephony. The sounds sent across the telephone wire by the transmitter could be faint and staticky.

THE DEVELOPMENT OF TELEPHONES WITH SEPARATE TRANSMITTERS AND RECEIVERS MADE THE INSTRUMENTS EASIER TO USE—CALLERS NO LONGER HAD TO KEEP MOVING A SINGLE PIECE OF EQUIPMENT FROM MOUTH TO EAR AND BACK AGAIN.

Sometimes spoken words were barely comprehensible. But Bell and Watson kept experimenting, improving the mechanism and extending the transmission over longer distances. By December 1876 they succeeded in sending an audible message over a distance of more than 140 miles (225.4 kilometers). The next month Bell patented a new design for a combined transmitter/receiver, one that used magnets instead of electromagnets. And in May 1877, the Bell Patent Association—soon to be formally renamed the Bell Telephone Company—offered the first telephones for public use.

But the Bell company did not sell telephones. Instead, it leased the machines for an annual fee, with an additional fee for running a line between two machines. The initial cost of a year's lease of two telephones "for social purposes" was twenty dollars. Phones leased "for business purposes" cost twice as much. The lease arrangement established a business model that the telephone company would follow for decades.

Most of the early telephone customers were businesses, such as a fire alarm company and the water company of Cambridge, Massachusetts. The first private residential line ran from the office of Charles Williams, owner of the electrical shop where Bell's equipment was made, to his house, which was 3 miles (4.8 kilometers) away. Other business and private customers followed, in New England and elsewhere. In addition to leasing the machines, the Bell company licensed other newly formed companies to offer telephone service. Under this arrangement, the Bell Telephone Company gave these local companies the right to distribute equipment and set up lines for a fee. The first local phone company was incorporated in New York in August 1877, by which time a total of nearly eight hundred telephones were in use on the East Coast. The Bell Telephone Company also sold shares of stock in the company to the public as another way of raising funds.

Bell married Mabel Hubbard in July 1877, after receiving five thousand dollars from a Rhode Island businessman for a share of future telephone business in England. Soon afterward the newlyweds left for a

MABEL AND ALEXANDER GRAHAM BELL POSED FOR THIS PHOTOGRAPH MANY YEARS AFTER THE INVENTION
OF THE TELEPHONE ALLOWED BELL TO MARRY MABEL, THE DAUGHTER OF ONE OF HIS BUSINESS ASSOCIATES.

year-long trip to England and Scotland to promote telephony there. While in England, Bell demonstrated the telephone in a variety of places, including a coal mine, a diving suit submerged in the Thames River, and one of Queen Victoria's homes. The telephone caused such a sensation in England that composers William Gilbert and Arthur Sullivan even referred to the machine in their wildly popular 1878 operetta *H.M.S. Pinafore.* Back home, though, the Bell Telephone Company was running into trouble.

It started with William Orton and Western Union. The telegraph giant had missed its chance to own the telephone, and now people were beginning to realize that this new form of communication could become a major industry. Western Union decided to correct its mistake by jumping into the telephone business on its own. Orton hired Elisha Gray and Thomas Edison to develop their own versions of the telephone. They succeeded. In fact, Edison's transmitter/receiver (or transceiver), which used compressed carbon instead of an electromagnet to modulate the electric current, was better than Bell's—but it still used the principles of telephony that Bell had patented.

In 1877 Orton, in partnership with Gray, Edison, and others, formed the American Speaking Telephone Company to manufacture phones and lease them for use with Western Union's telegraph lines. Within less than a year, Western Union had connected more than 30,000 customers. Orton and his agents also began a campaign to smear Bell's reputation with articles and letters claiming that he was not the true inventor of the telephone but had stolen others' ideas or had obtained his patents through fraud or by bribing employees of the Patent Office. All the while, Western Union and the Bell company were racing to extend telephone service into new markets, such as the western states. The two companies competed bitterly for customers. Western Union had the advantage of a ready-to-use system of telegraph poles and lines; Bell had to string its own lines. And while the Bell company was still struggling to pay its bills, Western Union was worth about $41 million.

The telegraph company began buying up shares of Bell company stock, determined to put its rival out of business.

Bell was appalled by the ugliness of the fight. He wrote in disgust to Mabel, "The more fame a man gets for an invention, the more does he become a target for the world to shoot at." But her father, Gardiner Greene Hubbard, a businessman and an attorney, was determined to fight back. In the fall of 1878 the Bell Telephone Company filed a lawsuit against Western Union for violating the Bell company's patent rights. If Bell won the suit, Western Union would have to abandon its telephone business. If Western Union won, the Bell Telephone Company would probably be finished, because it could not afford to compete with Western Union for business. But waging a lawsuit was expensive, and the Bell company's funds were already nearly exhausted. The Bell partners decided to give up control of the company to new investors who could put more money into it. A group of Boston businessmen kept the Bell Telephone Company afloat financially and became its new directors.

As the two sides in the patent lawsuit began marshaling witnesses, taking statements, presenting evidence to the court, and in general preparing for the showdown to come, observers began to see that the Bell company—the puny David that had taken on the corporate Goliath—had a good chance of defeating the mighty Western Union. Bell made a convincing witness. His memory was excellent, and his record keeping was meticulous; he produced letters and other documents that detailed the time line of his work on the telephone. One of the most damning pieces of evidence Bell produced was an 1877 letter from Elisha Gray in which Gray said that he did not claim to be the inventor of the telephone because he had produced only an idea, not a practical model. According to some accounts of the case, when Gray's attorney asked him in court whether the handwriting on this all-important letter were really his, Gray said ruefully, "I'll swear to it—and you can swear at it!"

ELISHA GRAY, ONE OF BELL'S CLOSEST COMPETITORS IN THE RACE FOR NEW TELEGRAPHIC AND TELEPHONIC INVENTIONS, TRIED TO FILE PAPERWORK CONCERNING A TELEPHONE INVENTION AT THE U.S. PATENT OFFICE—BUT BELL'S PATENT WAS FILED SEVERAL HOURS EARLIER. GRAY'S BACKERS FOUGHT BELL'S CLAIM IN A BITTER COURTROOM BATTLE THAT LEFT BELL THE VICTOR.

By November 1879, before the case was fully presented to the court, Western Union's head attorney was convinced that his client could not win the suit. On his advice, Western Union made a settlement with the Bell company out of court. Western Union acknowledged the validity of Bell's patent and gave up its attempt to enter the telephone business. Western Union also turned over to Bell all of its telephones, telephone lines, and patent rights in telephony, including Edison's compressed-carbon transceiver. The Bell company, in turn, agreed to stay out of the telegraph business and to pay Western Union 20 percent of the money earned by its telephones for the next seventeen years—the lifetime of the Bell patents.

The settlement was a triumph for the young Bell Telephone Company, which now controlled a monopoly in a fast-growing industry with great potential for profit. Already, though, the original partners—Sanders, Hubbard, Bell, and Watson—were being driven out of the company.

Thomas Sanders had invested about $100,000—a large fortune for the time—in the telephone before it started to make money. To regain his losses, he sold his share of the Bell Telephone Company while the company was still new. Gardiner Greene Hubbard served as president of the company for a short time, until 1879, when the new directors replaced him with a businessman named William Forbes. Thanks to Hubbard's involvement in Bell Telephone, he remained comfortably wealthy until his death in 1897. Thomas A. Watson worked for the Bell company for just four years. In 1881 he left his position to devote himself and the earnings from his Bell shares to marriage, farming, and a variety of interests, investments, and activities that ranged from reincarnation to gold mining and acting.

Alexander Graham Bell left his job with the Bell company even earlier, in 1880, after disagreements with Forbes. He and Mabel had sold most of their Bell shares by 1883. If the Bells had held on to the shares longer, they would have risen greatly in value, but even as it was, the

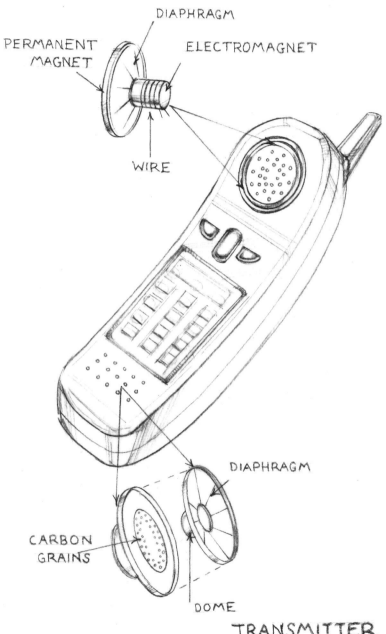

RECEIVER

PERMANENT
MAGNET

DIAPHRAGM

ELECTROMAGNET

WIRE

DIAPHRAGM

CARBON
GRAINS

DOME

TRANSMITTER

How a Telephone Works

The carbon transmitter used in today's telephones is much like the one that came into use in the late nineteenth and early twentieth centuries. It is a compartment filled with grains or crystals of carbon. One side of the compartment is attached to a diaphragm, a thin sheet or membrane of aluminum. A small dome in the center of the diaphragm protrudes into the carbon grains. When a caller speaks into the transmitter, his or her voice creates acoustic waves that move through the air and press against the highly sensitive diaphragm. The acoustic waves move the diaphragm, causing the dome to press against the carbon and then relax. These changes in pressure correspond to changes in the length of the acoustic waves carrying the speaker's voice. Because carbon crystals conduct more electric current when they are closely compressed than when they are more loosely packed, the movements of the diaphragm against the carbon create variations in the electrical current that is passing through the machine. Those variations in current exactly mirror the changes in the tone and pitch of the speaker's voice—or of any sound. In this way, the transmitter turns sound into electricity.

The electrical signal passes along the line until it reaches the telephone receiver. There it passes through another diaphragm. This diaphragm is made of iron and is attached to two magnets. One is a permanent magnet, which exerts a steady pull on the diaphragm. The other is an electromagnet, which is only magnetized when electricity flows through it. As the irregular pulses of the signal pass through the electromagnet, it exerts a constantly varying degree of magnetism. When the pull is strong, the electromagnet moves the iron diaphragm away from the permanent magnet; when the force is weak, the diaphragm moves back toward the permanent magnet. These back-and-forth movements push against the air next to the diaphragm, creating acoustic waves that match those spoken into the transmitter at the other end of the line. Electricity has thus been turned back into sound and can be heard by the listener.

couple and their children lived very well, with homes in Washington, D.C., and Canada. Bell never worked again. He remained actively interested in science and technology, and he invented a number of machines, although none was as important or profitable as the telephone. He designed experimental aircraft and helped to found the National Geographic Society. Bell also returned to his first and greatest passion when he founded the American Association for the Promotion of the Teaching of Speech to the Deaf.

Although Bell had left the telephone company, he had not said goodbye to the disputes, lawsuits, and controversy that plagued its early years. The Western Union lawsuit was the first major challenge to Bell's patents, but it was not the last. Alexander Graham Bell and the Bell Telephone Company would spend nearly two decades defending the Bell telephone patents against almost six hundred lawsuits from rival companies and inventors. The constant attacks angered and exhausted the inventor. Most painful and wearying to Bell, because it called his character into question, was the suit brought against Bell in 1885 by the Pan-Electric Company of Tennessee. Pan-Electric charged that Bell had used bribery and fraud at the U.S. Patent Office to "steal" the telephone patent from Elisha Gray. Although the case dragged on until 1892, Bell won it. In fact, he and the Bell company won every one of the many lawsuits leveled against them in those early years.

While Bell was defending his patents in court, the telephone was transforming the business of communication. As telephones became more widely used, a series of technical improvements and innovations solved some of the problems of early telephony.

One major problem was poor sound quality. Early callers often had to shout as loudly as possible to make themselves heard. Misunderstandings were common, as was frustration. Electricity itself, which had made the telephone possible in the first place, was part of the sound-quality problem. Electricity from many sources, including other telephone and telegraph lines, light and trolley lines, and lightning, could and did interfere with telephone signals. They turned attempts to communicate into "a jangle of meaningless noises," as Herbert Casson wrote in his 1910 book *The History of the Telephone.* "There were spluttering and bubbling, jerking and rasping, whistling and screaming. . . . There were clicks from telegraph wires, scraps of talk of other telephones, and curious little squeals that were unlike any known sound." Making higher-quality telephone wires out of copper and insulating them with rubber helped combat the interference. So did the improved form of the telephone, using a carbon transmitter, that came into general use around 1882.

The carbon transmitter, which was a form of microphone, sent sound more clearly and accurately than Bell's first transmitters. Instead of relying on a weak magnet-induced current, like Bell's early models, the carbon transmitter used a strong electrical current sent through the wire that connected the transmitter and the receiver. This made the telephone a bit more expensive to operate, but much more effective for its intended use—communication.

But a telephone, no matter how efficient, is no good to just one person. Every conversation needs two sides. Connecting people was one of the major challenges of early telephony. At the very beginning, Bell and his partners simply strung a line between any two telephones leased by a customer, or between any two customers who wanted to be linked. Most of the first customers were businesses or professional offices—doctors, for example, were quick to see the advantages of being linked to drugstores. One of the first Americans to have private telephones installed in their houses was writer Mark Twain, who lived in Hartford, Connecticut. He had a direct line to the local newspaper, the *Courant.*

The method of connecting each pair of telephones with a line could not continue, of course. Telephone customers wanted to be able to call more than one other location, but it was impossible to imagine every telephone linked to every other phone by a direct line—the massive tangle of wires would bury a town. Fortunately for the future of the telephone, a better solution appeared.

It originated in the offices of E. T. Holmes, owner of a burglar-alarm company in Boston. Holmes, one of Bell's earliest commercial customers, leased telephones and lines to connect all of his clients to his office. All of the lines entered his office near the same point, resulting in a bank of telephones placed side by side. Someone operating the phones in the office could move from one to another. From this arrangement came the idea for the switchboard, a hub through which all lines would pass, where a call from any telephone could be connected to any other receiver. The term *exchange,* which referred to a point where telegraph messages were retransmitted or rerouted, was adopted for this new center of telephone-line linking.

The first commercial telephone exchange was installed in New Haven, Connecticut, in January 1878—but not by the Bell company. Bell's arch-rival Western Union created it for fifty subscribers. Similar exchanges soon sprang up in every community that had telephones. By 1887 the United States had more than a thousand exchanges serving a total of more than 150,000 subscribers. All of the exchanges worked in the same basic way. A line ran from each telephone customer to the exchange. A customer who picked up a telephone to make a call was connected to the exchange, where an operator answered. The customer gave the operator the name of the person he or she wanted to call. The operator then called that line and, if the call was answered, used a short, flexible cord with a plug on each end to connect the line of the incoming call to the line that ran to the receiving phone. Telephone numbers soon replaced the use of names at exchanges.

Central switchboards did not eliminate one growing problem, though: the clutter of telephone poles and lines. Every telephone had a line running to the switchboard at the exchange. Quickly the forest of poles and the spiderweb of lines became a nuisance, a safety hazard, or, at the very least, an unsightly mess, especially in populous cities. Some city blocks had thirty or more poles, and some poles carried a hundred wires. An extreme example of the problem was Wall Street, the heart of New York City's financial district, where dozens of 90-foot (27.5-meter) poles had thirty crossbars each and held three hundred wires aloft. The

BY THE END OF THE NINETEENTH CENTURY, TELEPHONES ADORNED WALLS IN THE EASTERN UNITED STATES AND PARTS OF EUROPE. CALLERS SPOKE INTO THE TRANSMITTERS THROUGH THE CYLINDERS MOUNTED ON THE FRONT OF THE MACHINES WHILE HOLDING THE CONE-SHAPED RECEIVERS TO THEIR EARS.

BEFORE INDIVIDUAL TELEPHONE LINES WERE GROUPED INTO CABLES, MASSES OF WIRES DARKENED BUSY INTERSECTIONS. THEY ALSO CREATED HAVOC WHENEVER A POLE TOPPLED.

weight of added lines just increased the risk of a storm or other calamity toppling one of the poles and pulling down the entire network.

One solution was to replace individual wires with cables, tightly wound bundles of wires that ran between poles. Individual lines to subscribers' houses or businesses could be connected to the cables instead of to the switchboards. In this way, just a few poles could serve a city block. Sometimes poles were not needed at all—the first underground telephone cables were laid as early as the late 1870s. Another solution was to make each existing telephone line carry more than one conversation at a time. By 1918 inventors had developed a technology known as frequency multiplexing (also sometimes called carrier telephony). Frequency multiplexing takes advantage of the fact that an electrical circuit can carry different frequencies at the same time. Acoustic signals from many telephones can be transmitted along a single line because each is paired with a carrier wave, an electrical current with its own frequency. At

the receiving end, the carrier frequencies are filtered and then stripped away from the acoustic signals. Such advances slowed the assault on America's forests. In 1885 alone, in the state of Vermont, more than 45,000 trees had been harvested for use as telephone poles. The need for poles continued, but not at the mad rate of the years before cables and multiplexing.

"Time and Distance Overcome" proclaimed an early advertisement for telephone service in Canada. True, the telephone was a much faster means of communication than the mail or the telegraph. But had it really overcome the barrier of distance?

A long-distance line was set up between Boston and New York in 1884. Within just a few years, other lines connected cities up and down the East Coast, from Albany, New York, to Washington, D.C. In 1893 the longest telephone connection possible was the 1,200-mile (1,932-kilometer) distance from Boston and Chicago. But it was not a very good connection, because the frequencies of a telephone signal became distorted as the signal traveled across great distances. By the time a sentence spoken in Boston reached a receiver in Chicago, the listener might hear only a garble of whistling and roaring sounds, not understandable speech.

In 1900 an American physicist named Michael Pupin discovered that placing electromagnetic coils at intervals along a telephone line eliminated distortion. With that problem solved, long-distance telephony advanced westward across the United States. Less than a dozen years later, though, progress halted again. The problem now was not distortion but a simple weakening of the signal over distance. It seemed that no call could reach farther than the distance from Boston or New York City to Denver, Colorado.

The solution to this new obstacle was the three-element vacuum tube, developed by Lee de Forest, an inventor working in California. The device was a sealed glass bulb containing electrical filaments in a vacuum, or state of complete airlessness. Passing a signal through the tube several times—a process called looping—boosted or amplified the signal's strength. So vacuum tubes were installed along long-distance lines. Called repeaters, they

LEE DE FOREST INVENTED THE VACUUM TUBE THAT IMPROVED LONG-DISTANCE TELEPHONY AND ALSO FIGURED IN THE DEVELOPMENT OF RADIO, TELEVISION, AND COMPUTERS. DE FOREST WAS A BRILLIANT INVENTOR BUT A POOR BUSINESSMAN; IN 1913, PLAGUED BY FINANCIAL TROUBLES, HE SOLD HIS VALUABLE PATENT TO THE BELL SYSTEM FOR ONLY $50,000.

were so effective at amplifying a telephone signal that only three were needed to boost a call from one coast of the United States to the other.

These developments allowed the Bell company to build the nation's first coast-to-coast telephone line, which required 130,000 telephone poles and 2,500 tons (2,268 metric tons) of copper wire. The line ran from San Francisco through Salt Lake City, Denver, Chicago, and Buffalo, then split into two branches that ran to Boston and New York City. It was completed and tested late in 1914. On January 25, 1915, Alexander Graham Bell in New York and Thomas Watson in San Francisco inaugurated the line with the first public coast-to-coast call. Bell repeated the famous words that had summoned Watson from the next room almost forty years earlier: "Mr. Watson—come here—I want to see you." To which Watson replied, "It would take me a week to get to you this time."

A telephone crew in Wisconsin in 1914, the year the first transcontinental phone line was completed. Linemen were among those who found jobs in the new field of telephone service.

Telephone Culture

"The world was not to be the same again," historian David McCullough has said about the invention of the telephone. "One small contrivance, considered at first to be a toy, became almost overnight universally indispensable."

Some people did think of the telephone as merely a toy—at first. In 1878 an editorial writer for the *New York World* wondered what possible use the new invention could be, then conceded that it might come in handy now and then for urgent affairs of state, or for marriage proposals by men too shy to speak up face-to-face. To many, the early telephones seemed only a scientific curiosity or an entertaining novelty. A few people even worried that the new devices might be the tools of supernatural powers such as ghosts or demons. But as telephone poles proliferated along streets and roadways, people realized that the new instrument was changing more than the landscape. It was changing lives.

The telephone created new job possibilities. Workers who installed telephone lines on rooftops or strung them from pole to pole were called linemen. Their challenging job required them to face all kinds of weather and terrain. Before safety equipment became standard, the job was also dangerous. Linemen worked atop tall poles or on high buildings, handling high-voltage electrical wires. Falls and electrocutions, some of them fatal, occurred.

Demanding in a different way was the job of the switchboard operator. The first operators were boys and young men, most of whom had worked as telegraph messengers. These youths were "an instant and memorable disaster," wrote John Brooks in *Telephone: The First Hundred Years.* Boisterous and bored with the work at the telephone exchange, they fought among themselves and treated customers rudely, swearing at them or prankishly misdirecting their calls. Angus Hibbard, an early Bell manager, later recalled the complaints of indignant customers, saying that "a great cry for help rose up throughout the land." Assistance came in the hiring of female operators, who were expected to be better behaved and more refined.

Emma Nutt of Boston was the first woman hired by the Bell company, for whom she worked from 1878 until her retirement in 1911. Others quickly followed. Within a year or so, the tumult of the "telephone boys" had faded, and discreet politeness reigned in every telephone exchange. By that time, virtually all switchboard operators were women.

Not just any women. The telephone company hired only those who were single—an operator who married would lose her job. The operators had to wear long dark skirts and white shirts with linen collars. They were expected to sit upright with perfect posture, wearing transmitters and receivers mounted on harnesses that rested on their shoulders, plugging and unplugging lines for nine hours a day, six days a week. Supervisors drilled them in the pronunciation of the proper phrases to use with customers. The supervisors also kept an eye out for such forbidden acts as crossing the legs or blowing the nose without permission.

By today's standards, those old rules regulating the conduct of women operators are not just outdated and unbelievably strict but, in some cases, illegal. Yet they were a reflection of the times, when workdays were long and employees' privileges were few. It was still rare in those days for women to work outside the home; when they did, they

BY THE MID-TWENTIETH CENTURY, TELEPHONE-EXCHANGE WORKERS WERE NO LONGER GOVERNED BY THE STRICT RULES THAT HAD REGULATED THE EARLY "SWITCHBOARD GIRLS." STILL, SWITCHBOARD OPERATION REMAINED A LARGELY FEMALE PROFESSION.

not only made less money than men but faced closer scrutiny in the workplace. No one, however, argued with the fact that women operators brought order and calm to the chaotic realm of the telephone exchange.

Urban exchanges became busy places, with dozens of women working at top speed. Efficiency was a key virtue. Chatting with the callers was forbidden—"if you got caught talking with a customer, that's one mark against you," one veteran operator reported. Rural exchanges, though, were another matter entirely. "While the city operator was an anonymous voice with scripted words, her country cousin was anyone willing and able to handle the board and, most likely, someone everyone knew," according to Ellen Stern and Emily Gwathmey in *Once Upon a Telephone: An Illustrated Social History*. "She might be Daisy, the farmer's daughter, propped on a milking stool, flipping the switch for her father's independent exchange, or Miss Evelyn, whose omniscient position confirmed her status as the most powerful member of the community. Messenger and muse, eager to help by knowing everybody's business, she mediated marital mishaps and party-line disputes, reported the weather, announced train schedules and delays, pacified panicky children, shared recipes for blueberry crunch, and saved lives."

Not everyone was a fan of the "switchboard girl." Almon B. Strowger, an undertaker in Kansas City, became convinced that the operators at the local exchange were routing his customers to a rival business. Strowger vowed to invent a "girlless" telephone exchange, one that would operate with mechanical fairness rather than human favoritism, and he succeeded. In 1889 Strowger produced the first automatic switching mechanism, which used a system of small motors and levers to connect calls—customers entered the desired number by pushing buttons on their telephone sets. Strowger's innovation led the way to both the automatic exchange and the dial telephone (even after pushbutton phones were reintroduced in 1964, people continued to speak of "dialing" a telephone number). Although dialing was both quicker and more private than operator-directed calling, it took time to convert the telephone system to automatic calling. Not until 1921 did the first fully automatic exchange—located in Omaha, Nebraska—go into service. In the decades that followed, automation gradually took over most of the tasks once performed by human operators. Still, even with today's nearly complete automation of call switching, operators remain on duty as troubleshooters and problem solvers.

Early telephone users grappled with a perplexing array of vexing questions about phone etiquette and customs. One question arose at the very beginning of the telephone age: when your phone rings, how should you answer it? Alexander Graham Bell always answered by saying, "Ahoy-hoy" into the speaker; he hoped that would become the standard response. Rival inventor Thomas Edison favored "Hello," which proved to have greater staying power. But Bell's distinctive salutation left a legacy in popular culture: C. Montgomery Burns, the villainous and antiquated power-plant owner on television's animated series *The Simpsons*, invariably answers his telephone by bleating, "Ahoy-hoy."

Other pressing questions concerned how and when to use a telephone, or even who should use one. At the dawn of the telephone age, a few writers had speculated that political leaders might find the new device useful, and eventually the telephone did come in handy for affairs of state. In 1879 Rutherford B. Hayes became the first U.S. president to have a telephone in the White House. As soon as it was installed, Hayes placed a call to Alexander Graham Bell. The first presidential words uttered into the telephone were, "Please speak more slowly." Presidents Theodore Roosevelt (1901–1909) and Woodrow Wilson (1913–1921) disliked the contraption and used it only when absolutely necessary. Herbert Hoover, who took office in 1929, was the first president to install a telephone on his desk and use it frequently.

Some people thought that while it might be all right for men to use phones, especially for business or government purposes, there was

WHO SHOULD BE ALLOWED TO USE TELEPHONES, AND WHEN? IN THE EARLY DAYS OF TELEPHONY, SOME DOUBTED THAT IT WAS PROPER FOR WOMEN AND CHILDREN TO USE THE NEW MACHINES.

something vaguely indecent about women sending their voices out into the world on the new contraption. Others saw nothing wrong with housewives—or their servants—using the telephone for practical things, such as ordering groceries or summoning a doctor to a sick child, but thought it rude to use a phone for personal communication. Some people were so proud to have a telephone that they had the machine installed in the front hall or parlor of their house; others hid it away. A 1917 guide to home decoration recommended the secretive approach: "Another hall abomination is the telephone. Unless we want our guests to know the price of their roast, or the family to listen in aghast while we tell a white lie for society's sake, or the cook to hear us asking for a new one's references, don't put your telephone in the hall. Closet it, or keep it upstairs, where the family alone are the bored 'listeners in.'"

But by 1922, when a magazine article on etiquette reported that several high-society matrons had recently used telephones to invite guests to parties, snobbish resistance to the phone was fading fast. The telephone company—which naturally wanted more people to use telephones in more ways—used various forms of advertising to convince the public of the virtues of telephony. It printed Christmas cards with telephones on them and passed them out for people to use. "I'd like to call you up to say 'Merry Christmas,'" reads one such card, suggesting that the sender wants the recipient to get a telephone. A poster showed a well-dressed woman trying to step across a puddle of rain, her umbrella ripped to shreds by the wind. The accompanying text reads: "In stormy weather, use the telephone." And "Just 30 minutes and my luncheon's all arranged," a beaming hostess tells a friend in another advertisement as she brandishes a telephone receiver. The telephone company also instructed customers on the proper way to speak into a transmitter (with your mouth next to the machine) and how to hang up a receiver (gently—slamming it down was said to be as rude as slamming a door).

Telephones had arrived, bursting into popular culture, appearing in cartoons, songs, plays, movies, and novels. They were symbols of communication, in all its good and bad aspects. The telephone could be a symbol of longing and touching emotion, as in the sentimental song, "Please, Miss, Give Me Heaven," written around 1890, in which a young child asks the switchboard operator to connect her with her dead mother. Hundreds and hundreds of songs about phones and calling soon followed, many of them comical.

Telephones have always lent themselves to comedy because of their potential for miscommunication. Overheard or misunderstood phone conversations, wrong numbers caused by overworked switchboard operators or misdialings, children's prank calls, and the supposed passion some teenaged girls had for chattering and giggling on the telephone for hours have all been the subjects of jokes, humorous songs and stories, and television sitcoms. For example, 1960's *Bye Bye Birdie,* a satire of American teenaged life and the teen idol Elvis Presley, included an elaborate production number called "The Telephone Hour," with about twenty young men and women yakking away in a web of overlapping calls.

Humor associated with the telephone also sometimes had an edge. For example, a 1905 postcard was titled "Tales the Telephone Girl Could Tell" and showed an operator listening in while two men talked about women who were clearly not their wives. The joke drew on two features of telephony that many viewed with alarm: the widespread practice, at the time, of eavesdropping on other people's conversations, and the tendency for people to use the telephone for less-than-respectable purposes.

Since the telephone's early days, it has been associated with romance—all kinds of romance, spanning the spectrum from innocent flirtation to seduction, and even adultery. Nineteenth-century songwriters and artists portrayed the telephone as "Cupid's Messenger." The love connection runs through the entire history of the telephone in popular culture, from a 1905 postcard of a smiling telephone operator

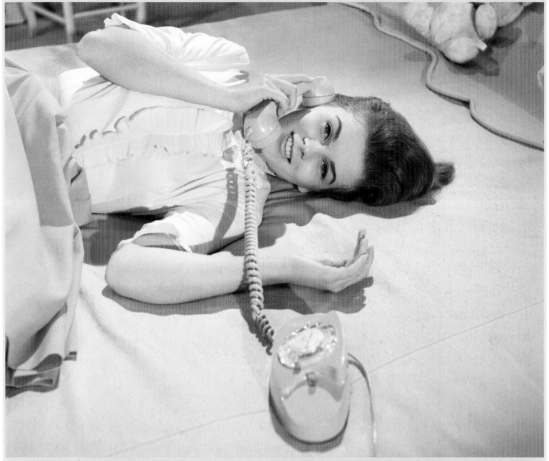

ACTRESS ANN-MARGRET IN A SCENE FROM *BYE BYE BIRDIE*, A MUSICAL AND MOVIE THAT FEA-
TURED TELEPHONE-OBSESSED TEENAGERS. BY THE 1960S, YOUNG PEOPLE HAD BECOME IMPORTANT
CONSUMERS OF TELEPHONE SERVICE.

making a date to Nicholson Baker's 1992 novel, *Vox,* a story of passion
between two people who are mistakenly connected by a wrong number.

Phones have played key roles on stage and screen. In the late nineteenth century and early twentieth centuries, musical comedies such
as *The Telephone Girl* and *Piquette* depicted the lives and loves of
swichboard operators. Gian Carlo Menotti's short 1947 operetta *The
Telephone* tells the story of a young man who wants to propose to his
sweetheart but cannot find a chance to do it because she is always
talking on the phone. In desperation, he goes to the corner store, calls
her, and proposes over the wire. (She accepts.) The 1967 television
drama *The Human Voice,* written by French playwright and director

THEODORE N. VAIL JOINED THE BELL COMPANY AS GENERAL MANAGER IN 1878 AND RAN IT UNTIL HIS RETIREMENT IN 1919, THREE YEARS AFTER THIS PHOTOGRAPH WAS TAKEN. VAIL TURNED THE BELL COMPANY INTO THE MASSIVE MONOPOLY KNOWN AS AMERICAN TELEPHONE AND TELEGRAPH (AT&T) AND DOGGEDLY PROTECTED IT FROM COMPETITORS.

Cellular showed a kidnapped science teacher using the pieces of a shattered telephone to establish a link with the cell phone of a possible rescuer.

Mark Twain, one of the world's first telephone customers, was a fan of progress and inventions; his 1876 book, *The Adventures of Tom Sawyer,* was the first novel to be written on a newfangled gadget called a typewriter. Yet Twain saw the humor—and the possible drawbacks—of telephony right from the start. He is reported to have said to the men who installed his telephone, "The voice carries entirely too far as it is. If Bell had invented a muffler or a gag he would have done a real service. . . . Put the thing near the window, so that I can get rid of it easily."

Despite all the jokes, the telephone has always had its practical and serious side. Its potential to save lives and property was clear from the beginning—the first commercial telephone installation, after all, was in a burglar-alarm company. People called switchboard operators in all kinds of emergencies, from sudden illness to fire, and the operators did their best to summon help. They also issued warnings to subscribers when they heard of dangerous weather. In 1921, for example, the operator of one rural Colorado switchboard called everyone on one side of town to warn them that a flood was headed their way. The telephone was a lifesaver in other ways, too. It gave invalids a link with the outside world. It ended the isolation of individuals who lived or worked far from others. Above all, the telephone eased the loneliness of people who were separated by distance from their loved ones. A postcard from the 1920s captured that aspect of telephony with the image of a phone sitting on a table next to an open window, with telephone poles and lines receding across the landscape of hills outside. The message reads:

> Let this picture bring to mind
> That where'ere your home is,
> You're only just as far from me
> As the nearest phone is.

THEODORE N. VAIL JOINED THE BELL COMPANY AS GENERAL MANAGER IN 1878 AND RAN IT UNTIL HIS RETIREMENT IN 1919, THREE YEARS AFTER THIS PHOTOGRAPH WAS TAKEN. VAIL TURNED THE BELL COMPANY INTO THE MASSIVE MONOPOLY KNOWN AS AMERICAN TELEPHONE AND TELEGRAPH (AT&T) AND DOGGEDLY PROTECTED IT FROM COMPETITORS.

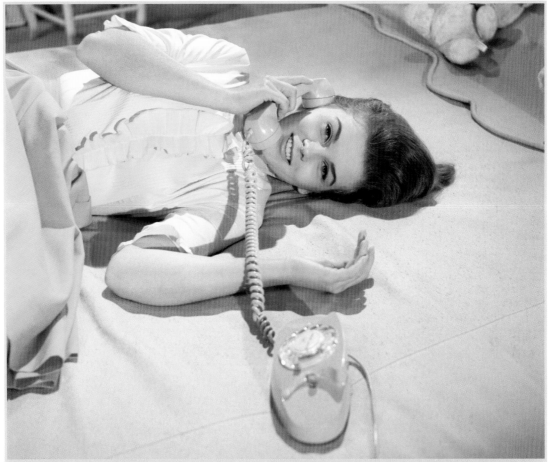

ACTRESS ANN-MARGRET IN A SCENE FROM *BYE BYE BIRDIE*, A MUSICAL AND MOVIE THAT FEA-TURED TELEPHONE-OBSESSED TEENAGERS. BY THE 1960S, YOUNG PEOPLE HAD BECOME IMPORTANT CONSUMERS OF TELEPHONE SERVICE.

making a date to Nicholson Baker's 1992 novel, *Vox,* a story of passion between two people who are mistakenly connected by a wrong number.

Phones have played key roles on stage and screen. In the late nine-teenth century and early twentieth centuries, musical comedies such as *The Telephone Girl* and *Piquette* depicted the lives and loves of swichboard operators. Gian Carlo Menotti's short 1947 operetta *The Telephone* tells the story of a young man who wants to propose to his sweetheart but cannot find a chance to do it because she is always talking on the phone. In desperation, he goes to the corner store, calls her, and proposes over the wire. (She accepts.) The 1967 television drama *The Human Voice,* written by French playwright and director

Jean Cocteau, features Swedish actress Ingrid Bergman as an emotionally disturbed woman clinging to her telephone as though it is a lifeline.

The sinister side of the telephone, its uses in double dealing and criminal plotting, came front and center in such movies as *Sorry, Wrong Number* (1948) and *Dial M for Murder* (1954). The shocking sound of a phone ringing was a central element in the 1979 suspense movie *When a Stranger Calls,* about a babysitter terrorized by anonymous calls. And for anyone who has ever heard a public telephone ringing and wondered who might be on the other end of the line, the 2002 thriller *Phone Booth* shows a man answering such a ring, only to be targeted by a crazed sniper in a nearby building. Two years later, the film

Ma Bell and Her Babies

After Alexander Graham Bell and his partners left the company they had founded, the telephone business in the United States went through a number of changes. Several of the most important stemmed from the work of Theodore N. Vail, whose decisions set the course that American telephony would follow through much of the twentieth century.

One of the last things Gardiner Greene Hubbard did before leaving the Bell Telephone Company in 1878 was to hire Vail, a postal official, as general manager of the company. Vail proved to be an outstanding business manager. Even after the company passed into the control of new owners, he remained in charge of its operations. Vail's great contribution to the company was strengthening the Bell monopoly.

The two original Bell patents, so long and earnestly attacked and defended in court, gave the company its initial monopoly. Once Bell had driven Western Union out of the telephone business, it was the only company that could legally sell, lease, or operate telephones in the United States. Local and regional telephone companies, of which there were many, had to operate under licenses from the Bell company. These licensees gave the Bell company shares of stock in their own companies, which meant that the Bell company ended up controlling between 30 and 50 percent of most of the licensees. This allowed the

AN EARLY DESK TELEPHONE. THE TRANSMITTER AND RECEIVER ARE STILL SEPARATE.

company to maintain tight control over the companies that did business in its name. Anyone who tried to operate a telephone business without Bell's license faced a patent-infringement lawsuit. But patent protection would not last forever—just for seventeen years. Bell's patents would expire in 1893 and 1894. After that time, anyone at all could copy Bell's invention and set himself up in the telephone business.

To keep the approaching expiration of the patents from dooming the Bell enterprise, Vail reorganized the company to meet the challenge. "What we wanted to do," he later explained, "was to get possession of the field in such a way that, patent or no patent, we could control it." One of his first steps was to speed up and improve the manufacture of Bell telephones, which were still being produced, too slowly to meet demand, in Charles Williams's Boston shop. In 1882 Vail bought Western Electric, a manufacturing firm founded by Elisha Gray and owned by Western Union. He turned it into a factory dedicated to making Bell telephones, switchboards, and other products. Three years later the main Bell company, now called American Bell but still based in Massachusetts, formed a New York company called American Telephone and Telegraph (AT&T) to develop a long-distance telephone network. As president of AT&T, Vail intended to keep the Bell system strong by practicing what students of business call vertical integration—the control of every aspect of a business by a single management. From planning the company's future moves to making the telephones, from stringing the wires to staffing the exchanges and supervising the licensees, the parent company did it all.

By 1893 the Bell company had about 230,000 telephones in operation across the United States. Then the Bell patents expired, and a telecommunications war erupted. The first such war had been between Bell and Western Union in the first few years of telephony, when Bell was the puny newcomer and Western Union was the mighty corporate giant. This time, though, Bell was the rich and powerful Goliath, attacked by a swarm of Davids.

Overnight, companies entered into competition with Bell. Some were wildcat operations, run on hope and shoestrings, that could not raise enough money to stay in operation and quickly fell by the wayside. Others were out-and-out frauds, run by con artists who took money for telephone deposits but never delivered lines or machines. But others dug themselves into the telephone business, chiefly in the South, Midwest, and West, generally in rural regions, where the Bell system had penetrated only sketchily, or not at all.

By this time, the Bell corporation's high rates and somewhat bullying approach to business, as well as its continued focus on the urban East Coast, had turned many Americans, especially those in the rural heartland, against the telephone giant. To emphasize their difference from Bell, the independent companies played up their folksy local identities with such names as the Home Telephone Company. They appealed to people's desire to own things by selling their telephones outright, rather than leasing them for a fee as the Bell system continued to do. They sought out customers on isolated farms and in small towns and villages. Some of the new phone companies, in fact, were run by farmers or ranchers who attached telephones and batteries to their fence lines and started small operations to serve themselves and their neighbors. Many of the independents barely scraped by—but they stayed in business. By 1897 these rivals numbered more than five thousand. They formed the National Independent Telephone Association to help each other resist Bell's drive to dominate.

The Bell system had more money, more experience, and better equipment than any of the independents. It also had a powerful weapon—it could and did refuse to link its telephone service with that of any unlicensed competitor. This meant that someone who subscribed to an independent telephone service could not call Bell customers. And because AT&T would not allow independents to link with each other through its own wires, the fledgling companies in different

INDEPENDENT TELEPHONE COMPANIES, MANY OF THEM FOUNDED AND RUN BY FARMERS WHO BROUGHT PHONE SERVICE TO THEIR RURAL DISTRICTS, SURVIVED FOR A TIME WHILE AT&T CONCENTRATED ON BUILDING ITS BUSINESS IN MAJOR CITIES.

LONG BEFORE THE MODERN CONFERENCE OR THREE-WAY CALL, TELEPHONING COULD BE A PUBLIC AFFAIR. PEOPLE SHARED CALLS ON SINGLE TELEPHONES, AND MULTIPLE HOUSEHOLDS SHARED PARTY LINES. PUBLIC TELEPHONES WERE STILL ENOUGH OF A NOVELTY THAT BYSTANDERS OFTEN EAVESDROPPED ON CALLS, REGARDING THEM AS FREE ENTERTAINMENT.

towns or regions usually could not interconnect. In areas where more than one company was active, telephone service became a confusing patchwork. People had to remember not just their friends' telephone numbers but what companies they used. Businesses had to subscribe to multiple services in order to be able to connect with all of their clients.

The Bell system continued to fight the independents in other ways. It improved service and equipment. Bell's rates had always been high, and the company was well established among the upper and upper-middle classes. Then, to lure less affluent customers, Bell lowered its rates in some areas. In addition, some of the Bell companies also pioneered new forms of service, such as party-line telephones that were cheaper than private lines and coin-operated pay phones in public places. But the Bell system's biggest advantage over the independents was long-distance service. Even when the smaller competitors pooled their resources, they could not compete effectively or profitably in an area of telephony that required heavy investment in technical research and in the contruction of long-distance telephone lines. AT&T tightened its grip on long-distance service by purchasing the patent rights to key innovations. In 1913, for example, when Lee de Forest, the inventor of the three-element vacuum tube, was facing legal and financial troubles, AT&T acquired his patent for this key element in long-distance telephony at the bargain price of $50,000.

Vail made sure that the ceremonial coast-to-coast telephone call between Bell and Watson in January 1915 produced a huge blitz of publicity for Bell and AT&T. Newspapers across the country reprinted the conversation between the two grand old men of telephony. Enthusiastic journalists made extravagant claims for the long-distance telephone, such as that it could have prevented the Civil War of the 1860s, or that it would unite the nation as nothing else had done. The general public was eager to begin long-distance calling, and almost at once it was able to do so, when the Bell system added branch lines and repeaters so that its exchanges could link to the transcontinental line. Many people concluded that this achievement in long-distance communication was enough of a justification for a single telephone system—in other words, for a monopoly.

And a monopoly was just what Vail had achieved. Less than a year earlier, in a 1914 deal with the federal government and the independent telephone companies, the Bell system agreed to let independents connect to its long-distance lines, in exchange for a share of the fees they collected. And where two or more phone services competed in local markets, Bell agreed to end the confusion by either selling its licensee companies to the competing independents or purchasing those independents (in practice this meant that Bell would buy up most of the independents, which could not afford to buy Bell companies). The result would be a single telephone company in each market, but even those companies that remained independent would have to cooperate with Bell to use its long-distance network. In an era when the federal government was busy enacting antitrust laws designed to break up monopolies, Vail managed to create an iron grip on the entire telephone industry. The Bell monopoly would last for decades.

Meanwhile, telephony advanced rapidly in the United States and around the world, thanks to technical advances and a growing customer demand for service. The first telephonic communication between North America and Europe was a call between two Bell engineers in 1915, one in Paris and the other in Virginia. Commercial telephone service between the two continents started twelve years later. Soon it spread to other continents. In 1935 two officials of the Bell system made the first round-the-world telephone call. They were in the same New York City building at the time—but the call was routed around the world, a distance of 23,000 miles (37,030 kilometers), between them.

Early international and intercontinental calls used radiotelephony, in which telephone signals were sent across the ocean on radio waves. Electrical storms, solar flares, and other atmospheric conditions frequently disrupted the radio portion of the connection, however. Not un-

FIBER-OPTIC LINES, WHICH USE PULSES OF LIGHT TO SEND SIGNALS, ARE REPLACING OLD TELEPHONE CABLES IN SOME PARTS OF THE WORLD.

til submarine telephone cables were laid in the 1950s did the service become more reliable. By then, though, a new radio technology was beginning to replace telephone cables on land. Microwave radio transmission uses high-frequency radio waves to carry all kinds of signals, including telegraph, telephone, and television as well as radio broadcasts. Lines of microwave receiver and transmitter towers, strung together according to the same relay principle that people like Claude Chappe had used in their pre-telephone signaling systems, could replace long-distance lines. The first microwave relay system came into use in 1947 between New York City and Boston, and it has grown steadily ever since. Although microwave radio frequencies also can be influenced by atmospheric electricity, the interruptions and distortions are much less noticeable than with the earlier radiotelephony.

Long-distance communication took a giant leap forward in 1962, when the United States launched *Telstar,* the first communications relay satellite, into orbit around Earth. Microwave signals beamed to the satellite could be retransmitted to distant locations on the planet. Many additional communications satellites have since been launched by governments and private companies, and a large portion of global communications now bounces off these orbiting relays. The overland line has not passed out of use, however. The communications industry has improved the speed and quality of overland lines and increased their carrying capacity with such high-technology innovations as fiber optics, which transmits signals in the form of light pulses. Networks of fiber-optic cables are being installed, usually underground, in many places.

Telephony was an international phenomenon almost from the start, but it developed along various courses in different countries. In some nations today, telephone systems are owned and operated by private companies, as in the United States. Elsewhere, the government runs the national telephone system. Even where telephone companies are privately owned, however, they are to some extent regulated by the government, which limits what they can do. In the United States, the

TELEPHONE STYLES CHANGED OVER THE YEARS. SOME CHANGES WERE FUNCTIONAL. FOR EXAMPLE, TRANSMITTER/RECEIVER HANDSETS REPLACED THE OLD SYSTEM OF SEPARATE MOUTHPIECES AND EARPIECES, AND TOUCH-TONE PUSH BUTTONS REPLACED ROTARY DIALS. OTHER DESIGN CHANGES REFLECTED THE MOVE TOWARD SIMPLER STYLES AND THE AVAILABILITY OF NEW MATERIALS SUCH AS PLASTIC. TODAY THE PROLIFERATION OF STYLES CONTINUES, WITH MAKERS OF CELL PHONES OFFERING A DIZZYING ARRAY OF DESIGNS AND FEATURES.

telephone industry is overseen by the Federal Communications Commission (FCC). It scrutinizes the business practices of telephone companies and ensures that they obey laws that apply to their services. An international agency also exists. Called the International Telecommmunications Union (ITU), it sets technical standards to ensure that all companies around the world can interconnect.

Throughout most of the twentieth century, the monopoly that Theodore N. Vail had forged controlled telephony in the United States. The Bell Telephone System determined what technical innovations would be introduced, and when. It owned all telephones, leasing them to customers and regularly introducing new styles, colors, and features so that users would replace their old phones. It had become the largest corporation in the world. To some people, the telephone company was "Ma Bell," a friendly entity that kept everyone in touch. To others, though, the Bell system was a domineering octopus, strangling innovation, stifling competition, and generally having its own way.

By about 1960, businesses that wanted to enter the communication industry on their own terms—such as by building and operating their own microwave relay systems—were ready to attack Ma Bell. They launched a series of antitrust lawsuits against Bell. Once again the Bell organization fought fiercely to protect itself. This time, however, it lost the fight. In 1974 the U.S. Department of Justice filed a major antitrust suit against AT&T, charging it with illegally maintaining a monopoly. The suit requested that the Bell system give up ownership of the Bell operating companies, the local and regional providers of telephone service. In 1982 the company settled the case by making an agreement with the Justice Department. Twenty-two local operating companies were divested, or separated, from AT&T so that they would operate independently. These operating companies—immediately dubbed "Baby Bells" by the media—had to grant rival long-distance companies access to their networks and customers. At once, new companies began competing for customers' business. The most profitable monopoly in corporate history had come to an end.

Ever since 1982, economists, social scientists, and historians of business have debated whether the divestiture of AT&T was a good or a bad thing, whether it benefited telephone customers or hurt them, and what its long-term effects will be. Many have observed that since the divestiture, a series of corporate mergers has joined telephone companies and other communications businesses into an ever-shrinking number of ever-larger corporations, perhaps leading to the rise of new monopolies.

But one thing is certain: The breakup of the Bell system and the scramble for long-distance business that followed the breakup were part of a telecommunications revolution that picked up speed in the final quarter of the twentieth century and is still roaring along today. Telecommunications consumers are now confronted with a dazzling and often confusing array of products, services, features, and providers. As a key piece of this array, the telephone is now used for much more than simply making calls. And it no longer necessarily sits on your desk or hangs on your wall—if you want, you can take it with you wherever you go. For better or worse, the invention of the cell phone has integrated the telephone more completely into daily life than Alexander Graham Bell ever dreamed possible.

WIRELESS COMMUNICATION USHERED IN A NEW ERA IN TELEPHONY. TODAY'S TELEPHONE CAN FIT IN YOUR POCKET AND TRAVEL WITH YOU WHEREVER YOU GO.

SEVEN

I Can Hear You Now

May 1996 was a busy and tragic month on the world's tallest mountain. Dozens of climbers toiled toward the summit of Mount Everest, eager to add their names to the list of those who have stood on the roof of the world. Some of them succeeded. Others turned back, perhaps to try another year. Many climbers were on the mountain when a massive storm wrapped Everest's flanks in snow. Among those trapped by the storm, as night fell, was Rob Hall, a mountain guide and leader of one of the climbing groups. Hall had a cell phone. Before he died—one of many who perished on Everest that night—he was able to speak with his pregnant wife thousands of miles away in their New Zealand home.

Rob Hall's final phone call, like the saga of Flight 93 on September 11, 2001, and countless new stories of rescues made and lives saved because someone had a cell phone, reminds us that we have access to a level of communication that would have seemed unthinkable back in the 1940s, when comic-strip character Dick Tracy sported a wristwatch communicator that was not even a telephone, just a two-way radio, a kind of miniature walkie-talkie. But the cell phone was not the telephone's first jump into new territory.

Starting in the mid-twentieth century, a parade of new machines, phone features, and services allowed people to use their telephones in new ways. These innovations were costly at first, developed mainly for use in business and government, but quickly came down in price so that a wider range of consumers could afford them. First came the answering machine, which ended an agonizing dilemma: Should I stay home and wait for a call, or go out and take a chance on missing it? If your phone rang when you were not home, the answering machine recorded a message from the caller. Later, many people replaced their answering machines with voice mail, a telephone company service that records incoming calls without the need for a machine. Phone companies also began offering callers other new services, such as call waiting, conference calling, and caller identification. Another device that made its way from the office to the home was the fax—or facsimile—machine, which converts a printed page into an electrical signal and sends it to another machine over a telephone line. Fax machines let people "phone" documents to one another. Cordless telephones let people talk on the phone from anywhere in their house or yard—anywhere, that is, within range of the line connection in the handset's base, about 65 feet (20 meters) or so.

In 1947 scientists at AT&T's Bell Labs invented the transistor, a compact device that amplifies and corrects an electrical signal. Transistors soon replaced bulky vacuum tubes in products such as radios, making them far more portable. Of course, AT&T also applied the transistor to telephone technology. By the late 1940s, it had developed car phones, portable radiophones for use in vehicles. The car phone let Americans combine two of their great passions, driving and talking on the phone. The instruments, however, were bulky and expensive, and they were not always reliable or user-friendly. AT&T worked on improving car phones, with the goal of putting one into every vehicle on the road, but before the car phone had become much more than a novelty, another company's technological breakthrough overshadowed it.

Between the early 1960s and the early 1980s, Motorola, a pioneer of radio and television technology, invested nearly $100 million to de-

A 1959 CAR PHONE. EARLY CAR PHONES WERE BULKY AND OFTEN WERE DIRECTLY ATTACHED TO THE AUTO-MOBILE. USED PRIMARILY IN BUSINESS AND IN THE MILITARY, THEY DID NOT CATCH ON AS WIDELY WITH THE PUBLIC AS THE CELL PHONE WOULD LATER.

velop a much smaller, more portable wireless telephone—the cellular telephone, or cell phone. The cell phone is essentially a two-way radio that lets the user communicate with the local telephone network. The term *cellular* comes from the cell, a service area that typically ranges from 1 mile to about 20 miles (1.6 to 32.2 kilometers) across. In each cell is a relay station containing a receiver and a transmitter. Cell-phone users link up with the local phone service through these stations; as they move from cell to cell, a switch inside the cell phone transfers the connection. All cell-phone users know what happens when they pass from a cell into an area not served by a station: "no signal."

Martin Cooper of Motorola invented the cell phone and placed the first call with it in 1973—to a rival inventor at Bell Labs. The original idea had been to sell or lease the cell-phone technology to AT&T, but the breakup of the Bell monopoly meant that other companies could offer cell-phone service themselves. First, though, stations had to be built, and regulatory agencies had to allocate a set of radio frequencies for cell-phone use. In 1982, the same year as the AT&T divestiture agreement, the FCC authorized the use of commercial cell phones in the United States. The first cell phones came on the market the next year. Although they cost about $4,000, weighed nearly 2 pounds (0.9 kilograms), and were half as large as a shoe box, they started to catch on.

Cell phones followed the same pattern as another revolutionary new product that entered the marketplace at around the same time: the personal computer. The Apple corporation began marketing personal computers for home or individual use in 1977; IBM followed with the PC four years later. Just as with personal computers, sales of cellular telephones rose dramatically when prices fell and the products became smaller and easier to use.

Cell phones (and new conventional telephones, too) have something else in common with personal computers. Both use some of the same technology. In fact, cell phones, like many other electronic devices today, contain minicomputers to perform certain functions, such as transferring the connection among cells. In phones as in computers, transistors have been replaced by smaller, faster, and more powerful microchips. Another thing cell phones borrowed from computers is digitalization, a form of encoding data for high-speed, high-volume, highly accurate transmission. In the 1960s scientists developed digital transmission to send data between computers; now it is increasingly used in other media, such as television and telephony. Digitalization occurs when any electrical signal—voice, picture, or data—is "sliced" into many separate segments called samples. Each sample receives a seven-unit binary code in the form of a series of 0's and 1's. The digital signal can be transmitted more clearly and accurately than a continuous, or analog, signal, which is not sliced into samples. When the digital signal reaches the receiver, the samples are combined and the signal is converted back into its original form.

The link between telephones and computers grew stronger with the rise of the Internet, the cyberspace realm that is reached through a combination of computer software and a telecommunications connection. People first got onto the Internet by plugging a telephone line into their personal computers, and millions of users still connect to the Internet over telephone lines, despite the increasing availability of cable and wireless connections. To complicate matters further, a recent development called computer telephony has begun to erase the distinction between personal computers and telephones. Known as VoIP, for Voice-over-Internet-Protocol, computer telephony lets individuals conduct spoken conversations over the Internet by equipping their computers with microphones, speakers, and the necessary software. Companies now offering long-distance VoIP claim that the service they provide should be governed by Internet regulations, but some people in the FCC and the telephone industry argue that it should be governed by the much stricter regulations and taxes that apply to telephone service. Like many other questions in the age of advanced telecommunications, this one is technologically complex and unlikely to be easily resolved.

While VoIP pioneers turn their computers into replacements for their telephones, cell phones are absorbing tasks once performed by

CAMERA PHONES, SOME OF WHICH CAN CAPTURE VIDEO ACTION AS WELL AS TAKE STILL IMAGES, ARE BECOMING COMMON—AND RAISING NEW ISSUES OF PRIVACY.

computers. Thanks to digitalization, tiny portable cell phones can now be used for written and visual communication as well as for conversation. Depending upon the services purchased, cell-phone users can surf the Internet, download their e-mail, read online magazines, check the stock market, and exchange text messages with other subscribers by using the phone's keypad as a tiny typewriter.

The cell-phone screen, once simply a display of call-related information, has become part of a camera with which users can send and receive still and video images. Although videophones have been around since the 1960s, allowing people to see as well as hear one another, they never became popular—perhaps because people didn't want to be broadcast sitting in front of their phones. The much newer cell-phone video technology, however, is as portable as the cell phone itself. Witnesses to crimes in progress have videotaped them on their cell phones—a boon to law enforcement. Other uses, though, are more problematic. Guests at preview screenings of new movies may now be asked to surrender their cell phones at theater entrances to prevent them from capturing bootleg copies of the films. And what about privacy? If someone uses a small, unobtrusive cell phone to video-record you without your permission or even your knowledge, have your rights been violated?

Cell-phone use is on the rise around the world. In developing nations and remote regions where traditional fixed-telephone service is not yet universally available, cell phones may bypass traditional poles, cables, and telephones entirely, if enough relay stations can be built. Buying a cell phone means sorting through many competing products and service plans, and using it means mastering an array of menus and features. Cell-phone users, though, are making their voices heard in the marketplace. Some companies are simplifying their service plans to meet consumer demand. In 2003 cell-phone users won a victory when the FCC required telephone companies to let customers take their phone numbers with them when they switched to a new carrier. Before

SOME REMOTE PARTS OF THE WORLD NOW HAVE CELLULAR TELEPHONE SERVICE WHERE NO PHONE SERVICE AT ALL EXISTED UNTIL RECENTLY. OBSERVERS OF TECHNOLOGY THINK THAT SOME SUCH PLACES MAY BYPASS LAND LINES, POLES, AND CABLES ENTIRELY.

that time, companies counted on the nuisance of getting a new number as a means of keeping some customers from switching.

Along with changes in telephone technology, new uses for the telephone have appeared over the past half century. Shopping by phone, which has been around since the nineteenth century but became very widespread in the 1970s, is undeniably convenient. In the comfort of home, a consumer pages through catalogs from favorite stores, then picks up the telephone to order the desired items or calls a restaurant to order the delivery of anything from a pizza to a twelve-course meal. (These days, the customer is equally likely to do his or her shopping and ordering over the Internet.) But just as the phone can bring the world to your door, it can throw open your door to the world. Telephone shopping's flip side is telemarketing, in which businesses call people and try to sell them products or services over the phone. Ironically, a large share of all telemarketing calls in the late 1980s and the 1990s were from long-distance telephone companies hoping to entice people to switch to their services. Fed up with what sometimes seemed like an endless stream of calls, almost all of them at dinnertime, consumers insisted on protection. Various states created databases in which people could register if they did not want telemarketers to call them, and in 2002 the federal government established a national do-not-call registry, with stiff penalties for telemarketers that violate it.

Innovations and new trends in telephony continue to raise challenging new questions. Some are issues of customs and manners, to be answered informally. A good example is the announcements, now common, that ask patrons of movie theaters and concert halls to turn off their cell phones before performances. Other telephone-related questions will be settled in the legislatures and the courts. Some places, for example, have already passed laws against talking on cell phones while driving, citing a link between telephone distraction and accidents.

Two examples of telephone-related controversy appeared on March 22, 2004, on the same page of the *Oregonian* in Portland. An article titled "Cell towers loom over history" told of a dispute between the federal

As cellular communication spreads, scientists have begun investigating the possibility that the frequencies cell phones use may be harmful to brain cells. Social critics are looking at cell phones, too, asking what we might be giving up in exchange for the promise of instant worldwide communication at all times.

and state governments over who decides how close microwave towers for cell-phone service can be built to historic buildings. "What's worse?" the article asked. "Not being able to get a cell-phone signal or spotting antenna towers looming over century-old houses, covered bridges, and cemeteries?" The second article dealt with efforts by the U.S. Department of Justice to expand its wiretap rights—under which law-enforcement officers may secretly listen in on calls made by suspects in certain types of crimes—to Internet-based communications technologies such as VoIP. "No one in the Internet world is going to support this," declared one Internet-phone executive. "It's counter to everything we've done to date in terms of building the Internet as a free, anonymous, creative place." But if the telephone and the Internet continue to merge, whose rules should rule?

The modern portable telephone has abolished the limitations of place. Even the area code, the part of a telephone number that once tied it to a specific city or region, is becoming meaningless as people carry their cell phones and numbers around the country and the world. The telephone user today can be in touch with anyone, anytime, just as easily from the beach as from the boardroom or the bedroom. Competing for customers, cell-phone companies advertise such features as clear reception and wide service coverage; one company has built an ad campaign around a service technician who pops up in unexpected places and speaks into his cell phone, asking, "Can you hear me now?" For more and more people, whether at work or off duty, at home or away, the answer is "yes."

Total communication is wonderful for parents who want to be able to keep in touch with their kids at any time, for commuters stuck in traffic, for anyone who needs help. But it also makes privacy more rare and precious than it has ever been—and not just the privacy of those who can be called at any time, but also the privacy of those around them, fellow bus passengers or shoppers in grocery checkout lines, forced to listen against their wills to loud, one-sided conversations. Columnist Ellen Goodman addressed this problem in an article titled "Please, stop forcing us to invade your privacy."

What was once a communications miracle—the ability to reach people anywhere in the world by means of something carried in a pocket—is now an everyday occurrence. Evolving telephone technology is blurring the boundaries between public and private life, making the world a smaller place, and changing the way people do business and conduct their personal relationships. Some things, though, have not changed since the beginning of telephony. One of the very first telephone customers, Mark Twain, told the telephone installers to put the machine near a window so he could get rid of it easily if it became too annoying. And today, as communications scholar Paul Levinson points out in *Cellphone,* you "always can choose to shut the cellphone off, and be no worse than any other human since the beginning of time."

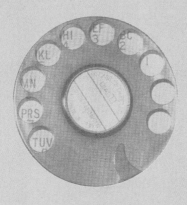

acoustics—The physical properties of sound; the science of sound.

cellular telephone, cell phone—A wireless portable telephone; the name comes from cells, the areas served by signal-relaying stations.

computer telephony—Spoken communication over the Internet, using computers fitted with microphones and speakers.

digitalization—The process of converting a sound or picture signal into sets of binary digits, the code system used to transmit computer data, and then back again into sound or picture.

microphone—An instrument that converts sound waves into electrical waves that can be transmitted or amplified.

monopoly—In business and commerce, the exclusive possession or control of a product, service, or commodity.

optical telegraph—An early form of long-distance communication that sent visual signals between towers or sighting stations.

party line—A type of telephone service, once common in parts of North America and some other regions, in which multiple households or users shared a single telephone line; typically, each user had a distinctive pattern of rings to indicate an incoming call.

receiver—In a telephone, the part of the instrument that turns electromagnetic signals into sounds; the earpiece or speaker.

switchboard—A device on which a number of different circuits, such as telephone lines, can be interconnected in various ways; a central hub for telephone connections.

telegraphy—The development and use of telegraph equipment; communication by telegraph.

telephony—The development and use of telephone equipment; communication by telephone.

transceiver—A unit that combines a transmitter and a receiver.

transmitter—In a telephone, the part of the instrument that turns sounds into electromagnetic signals; the mouthpiece.

VoIP—Voice-over-Internet-Protocol; see *computer telephony*.

ca. late 1700s
The word *telegraph* is created to describe a French long-distance communication system using semaphore.

1800
Alessandro Volta invents the electric battery.

1836
Samuel F. B. Morse builds a working model of his electric telegraph.

1844
Morse sets up the first public telegraph line, which links Baltimore and Washington, D.C.

1861
Western Union builds the first telegraph line across the United States. In Germany, Philipp Reis invents a machine that can send musical notes, and possibly human speech, over wires.

1872
Alexander Graham Bell begins trying to invent the multiple telegraph.

1874
Bell develops his first ideas about the electrical transmission of speech.

1875
Bell and his assistant, Thomas Watson, discover how to turn sounds into electric current, thereby inventing the telephone.

1876
On March 7, the U.S. government issues Bell his first telephone patent.

1877
The first commercial telephone system is installed in Charlestown, Massachusetts.

1893
A long-distance telephone line links Boston and Chicago.

1914
The Bell system of companies, headed by American Telephone and Telegraph (AT&T), establishes a monopoly on U.S. telephone service; the first transcontinental phone line across the United States is completed.

1921
Automated dialing systems are introduced.

ca. 1940
Microwave-radio relay systems are developed to carry telephone, telegraph, television, and data signals without wires.

1947
The first microwave relay system begins service between New York and Boston.

1962
Telstar, the first telecommunications satellite, is launched into orbit.

early 1960s
Transmission of computer data in digital form begins.

1973
Martin Cooper invents the portable handheld telephone, or cell phone.

1982
AT&T breaks up its telephone monopoly in a settlement with the Justice Department; the FCC authorizes commercial cellular-telephone service in the United States.

1980s
Fiber-optic technology improves high-speed data transmission.

ca. 2000
Cell-phone technology expands to include new features such as video transmission and Internet access; computer telephony begins.

Since this book was written, these Web sites may have changed, moved to new addresses, or gone out of existence. New sites may now be available.

The History of the Telephone

http://extext.lib.virginia.edu/toc/modeng/public/CasTele.html
A reproduction of Herbert N. Casson's 1910 *The History of the Telephone,* with anecdotes about Bell and the early years of telephone use.

About the Telephone

http://inventors.about.com/library/inventors/bltelephone.htm
A brief overview of telephone history, with related articles on key figures and on technological developments such as the cell phone.

Illustrated History

http://www.galaxyphones.co.uk/telephone_history02.asp
Sponsored by a British telephone company, this site offers a detailed account of telephone history and technology from the mid-nineteenth century, with numerous helpful diagrams and links to other sites.

Early Experiments with Telephony
http://www.ilt.columbia.edu/projects/bluetelephone/html/part1.html
A site that discusses inventors and experiments before Bell, during the period 1664 to 1866.

History of the Telegraph and Telegraphy
http://inventors.about.com/library/inventors/bltelegraph.htm
A brief overview of telegraph history, with related articles on Samuel Morse, aspects of telegraph technology, and a time line.

Adventures in Cybersound
http://www.acmi.net.au/AIC/TELEPHONE_FLAMMGER.html
A brief history of the telephone, with print references and a time line.

Bibliography

For Students

The American Experience: The Telephone. PBS Home Video, 1997.

Brooks, John. *Telephone: The First Hundred Years.* New York: Harper & Row, 1975.

Fisher, Leonard Everett. *Alexander Graham Bell.* New York: Atheneum Books for Young Readers, 1999.

Gearhart, Sarah. *The Telephone.* New York: Atheneum Books for Young Readers, 1999.

Grosvenor, Edwin S., and Morgan Wesson. *Alexander Graham Bell: The Life and Times of the Man Who Invented the Telephone.* New York: Abrams, 1997.

Levinson, Paul. *Cellphone: The Story of the World's Most Mobile Medium and How It Has Transformed Everything!* New York: Palgrave Macmillan, 2004.

Matthews, Tom L. *Always Inventing: A Photobiography of Alexander Graham Bell.* Washington, D.C.: National Geographic Society, 1999.

Pasachoff, Naomi E. *Alexander Graham Bell: Making Connections.* New York: Oxford University Press, 1996.

Skurzynski, Gloria. *Get the Message: Telecommunications in Your High-Tech World.* New York: Bradbury Press, 1993.

Stern, Ellen, and Emily Gwathmey. *Once Upon a Telephone: An Illustrated Social History.* New York: Harcourt Brace, 1994.

For Teachers or Advanced Readers
Bruce, Robert V. *Bell: Alexander Graham Bell and the Conquest of Solitude.* Ithaca, NY: Cornell University Press, 1990, 2nd ed.

Coll, Steve. *The Deal of the Century: The Breakup of AT&T.* New York: Atheneum, 1986.

Fischer, Claude S. *America Calling: A Social History of the Telephone to 1940.* Berkeley: University of California Press, 1992.

Katz, James Everett. *Connections: Social and Cultural Studies of the Telephone in American Life.* New Brunswick, NJ: Transaction Publishers, 1999.

Mackay, James A. *Alexander Graham Bell: A Life.* New York: J. Wiley, 1998.

Temin, Peter. *The Fall of the Bell System: A Study in Prices and Politics.* Cambridge, England: Cambridge University Press, 1987.

Page numbers for illustrations are in **boldface**.

About the Author

Rebecca Stefoff has written numerous nonfiction books for readers of all ages. Her works include biographies of historical and literary figures as well as books about science, nature, and exploration. Stefoff has written about discoveries and their effects in such works as *Charles Darwin and the Evolution Revolution* (Oxford University Press, 1996), and she is the author of the ten-volume Marshall Cavendish Benchmark series North American Historical Atlases and the five-volume World Historical Atlases series. You can find more information about her books for young readers at her Web site, www.rebeccastefoff.com